PENGUIN BOOKS

A CONSEQUENCE OF SEQUENCE

Idayu Maarof graduated with an M.D. from the Universiti Kebangsaan Malaysia medical school. She then served in several hospitals before starting her own general practice. Her interest in health care through patient education has resulted in her writing for magazines and her personal blog on healthcare issues such as how patients can make the best use of the medical infrastructure to their maximum benefit.

Dr Idayu Maarof is passionate about empowering the public with the knowledge to better enable them to cope with their health issues, believing that doctors should also teach and help patients manage their health, especially to prevent the onset of disease. She has given lectures and talks on a diverse range of healthcare issues, medical education and public engagement through medical writing. Her first book, *The Doctor is Sick*, won an Anugerah Buku Negara (National Book Award, Malaysia) in 2017.

Mohd Firdaus Raih is a bioinformatician and computational biologist by profession. He has published numerous research papers in peer-reviewed journals and chapters in books of high standing in the scientific community. He has also written widely on science and technology as well as higher-education issues in various newspapers and magazines.

T0124652

A Consequence of Sequence

The Aftermath of a
Life Seized by Two Tumours

By
Idayu Maarof
with
Mohd Firdaus Raih

PENGUIN BOOKS
An imprint of Penguin Random House

PENGUIN BOOKS

USA | Canada | UK | Ireland | Australia
New Zealand | India | South Africa | China | Southeast Asia

Penguin Books is part of the Penguin Random House group of companies
whose addresses can be found at global.penguinrandomhouse.com

Published by Penguin Random House SEA Pte Ltd
9, Changi South Street 3, Level 08-01,
Singapore 486361

First published in Penguin Books by Penguin Random House SEA 2021

ISBN 9789814914109

Typeset in Adobe Garamond Pro by Manipal Technologies Limited, Manipal

www.penguin.sg

To family

Contents

PART 3

PART 4

Preface

Writing a book about getting a sudden illness isn't something one ever plans to do. Even so, the personal notes I had kept of my sudden illness enabled me to tell the story from the perspective of a medical practitioner who was now the patient, not the healer. These notes were published as my first book, *The Doctor is Sick*.

Writing the book gave me closure. In some way, it also provided me with a sense of achievement and satisfaction. My ailment was not exactly common, so I had hoped my book would shed some light on such illnesses. My intent was that the words I had written could also help others. Not just those afflicted in the same way as I was, but also those who had suffered sudden and uncommon illnesses. I had hoped my story could provide hope to them and their caregivers.

After the first book, I had sort of gotten the writing bug. I had plans to write another book on some other subject matter. Obviously, my next book was not going to be about me being sick again. Unfortunately, things don't always go according to plan . . . such is the journey called life.

After I had finished most of the writing for *The Doctor is Sick*, I was again ill. This time, I was afflicted with almost daily seizures. Some of the episodes, rather uncommonly, lasted for hours. Because of these seizures, one of the options was to undergo brain surgery.

After my brain surgery, I decided that this was a story that I should also share with the hope that it could benefit others, especially patients suffering from epilepsy, brain tumours and other types of intractable and difficult-to-diagnose diseases. For me, it was a highly emotional journey for many reasons.

The story I narrate in this book is not just about me. It is also about my immediate family who were just as stricken by the illness as I was. It is about their distress at seeing me struggle every day, not knowing whether each time I closed my eyes to sleep would be my last time.

This book is told in a slightly different way compared to *The Doctor is Sick* because my recurrent bouts of seizures left me in a state of unawareness during those episodes, and it was my husband and sons who would relate these experiences to me. Thus, some parts of this book are told from my husband's point of view.

This book is about my illness and how I had coped. However, I caution those who may find themselves in what may seem to be a similar situation to not draw parallels but to instead seek out professional medical help. The opinions I put forth are my own and they may not reflect the opinions of others in the medical profession.

Idayu Maarof

PART 1

1

Visions of illusions

You know how sometimes you see bubbles and irregular shapes floating by in front of your eyes? Yet, they're not really there in front of you? These things have a technical medical term; they're called (*drumroll*) . . . 'floaters'—well obviously, what else could they be called?

We tend to see floaters especially when staring into the light or looking at something with a light background. However, when they never go away, then something may not be quite right with your vision. That was how it started for me. But I'm getting ahead of myself.

This story begins three months after I had an open-heart surgery. I needed the surgery to remove a tumour on my heart valve which was diagnosed as the probable cause for my multiple episodes of stroke.

The heart is basically muscle tissue that acts as a pump. The aortic valve, where my tumour was, is the doorway that controls the direction of blood flowing out of the heart. Because of the tumour sitting there, the blood flow was disturbed, thus resulting in clots or emboli. These clots were believed to be causing my strokes when they travelled via the bloodstream and became lodged in the brain.

The illness had been unexpected. I did not have any underlying or known factors that put me at high risk of a stroke. I had my first stroke in July of 2014. That same year, in October, I had an open-heart surgery to treat it. Although the journey felt long, the resolution to my illness was relatively quick. I was fortunate that I did not linger in an ill state for too long. Yes, there had been challenges before and after the heart surgery, but I had managed to overcome them, or at least thought I had. I wanted to slowly return to work despite being apprehensive about whether I would be able to practise medicine as I had done before the surgery.

The surgery to remove the tumour had gone without any untoward complications and I had recuperated well. The incision site wound had healed and my sternum (chest bone) seemed to have fused together again.

While recuperating from my heart surgery, I had kept notes of my experience of the whole ordeal. Since I thought I could offer a unique perspective as a medical doctor who had suffered strokes and had had to undergo open-heart surgery, I had organized those notes, with my husband's help, into a book entitled *The Doctor is Sick*. I was ready to move on. Life was ready to return to some semblance of normalcy, or so I had the audacity to presume.

After months of leaving the running of my medical practice to a colleague, I felt ready to work again. My cadre of doctors had also given their green light. Getting back to work was a significant milestone in my journey of healing. It was a sign that I had recovered and was ready to face life's other challenges and whatever future was in store for me. So back to my clinic I went. Then . . . it started.

One afternoon at my clinic, about three months after the surgery, I was doing some reading in between seeing patients when I noticed a sudden change in my vision, or perhaps lack of it. I simply could not clearly see what I was reading. The letters took on a reddish hue instead of the original black typeface as I moved from one word to another.

The words and sentences appeared to move and gradually float on to the surface of the paper. I began to see overlapping images and a fluttering effect, almost like a camera shutter trying to capture a high-speed event. Then there were also the floaters.

I blinked several times, followed by shutting my eyes, hoping that this would help it go away. Maybe it was because my eyes were tired? After all, I had been sitting in my consultation room since morning that day. I would usually walk around and chat with my staff when I was in between patients but, on that particular day, I had remained at my desk reading a book I was eager to finish.

Unfortunately, the problem persisted despite my efforts at resting my eyes. Was I seeing things? I tried to remain calm, but a sense of panic slowly crept in. After having experienced several strokes, my first thought was that this might be another one. I did not think that I was hallucinating. What I was seeing seemed to be real, very real, and it was not going away. It was a rather surreal experience.

I applied eye drops, hoping that it was just dry eyes. Then, I tried to take a short nap to give my eyes some rest after all the strain of reading. Unfortunately, my vision did not get back to normal. I still reassured myself that it was just my tired eyes and decided to ignore the symptoms I was experiencing. My gut feeling told me otherwise, but maybe I was in denial.

The reddish hue gradually disappeared, but the blurry double vision remained for a few more days. I had also become unsure of what one was supposed to see when one's eyes were closed. This was because I started to see a reddish hue even when my eyes were shut. I consoled myself that what mattered was my being able to see clearly every time I opened my eyes.

I remembered asking my husband regarding what he could see when he shut his eyes. Was it red or black? Or was it colours? His matter-of-fact answer was, 'Well, it's dark or black usually, but I can see a reddish hue if there is a strong light in the background.' I'm not sure if his answer helped, or made me even more uncertain. Of course, the fact that I was asking such questions made him worried and insistent that I see a doctor.

By then, my denial led me to simply attribute these symptoms to heightened senses because of the surgery. I dismissed what I was seeing as my being more aware of my surroundings, so much so that I could even make out minute differences of colour when I closed my eyes.

The heart tumour that led to an open-heart surgery had a huge impact on my life. The physical recovery was smooth sailing, but emotionally I was still fragile. The strength I showed was perhaps only superficial. The emotional scars of the illness ran deeper than the physical ones from the surgery.

Although I had no evidence of this, I suspected that my vision problems were of neurological origin, stemming from something in my brain, rather than my eyes.

After being in and out of hospitals due to the strokes and heart surgery, I was definitely not ready to get on that rollercoaster again, especially when I was ready to move on.

Trying to perhaps delay the inevitable, I sought the opinions of my medical school classmates through phone and text messages. They had mixed opinions of my symptoms. That was, of course, not unexpected because no one could physically examine me or conduct a proper diagnosis over the telephone. The general conclusion and consensus were that I needed to get myself properly examined in a setting that had proper access to diagnostic tools and facilities.

Perhaps I really was in denial as I was not sure I had the energy to face what I feared was happening all over again. Would I be able to cope with some new diagnosis? Would my family be able to take it?

The flow of diagnosis and treatment will generally be the same anywhere. To diagnose an illness, a doctor has to see the patient, get a proper history, and do a proper examination followed by investigations (if needed), before coming to a differential or final diagnosis. That is the basis of practising medicine.

I could not contain my worries any longer. Reluctantly and with dread, I decided to see my neurologist. I knew that she would probably not be best pleased that I had waited for so long before deciding to see her. Because of my history of strokes, I should have treated my visual problems with more urgency. There was always a possibility that it could have been something that could cause lasting damage if not treated early on.

Suddenly I was filled with regret. All the '*what-ifs*' came rushing across my mind as I awaited my turn in front of my neurologist's consultation room. *What if I had immediately gone to see the doctor? What if I had taken the symptoms more seriously? What if this was more serious? What if this was permanent?* . . .

2

Closure not

I had no scheduled appointment with my neurologist that morning. My recurrent stroke episodes had left me with sort of an open-as-required appointment status with her. She probably had an inkling that something was amiss when I had called for an urgent appointment and appeared at her clinic soon after.

'How are you?' she greeted me. 'Is everything all right?'

'It's my eyes . . .' I blurted out hurriedly. Then everything just came gushing out. I recounted my symptoms to her. She seemed worried about the new development and immediately referred me to an ophthalmologist—the obvious course since my problems seemed to be stemming from my vision.

When I went to see the eye doctor, most of the symptoms seemed to have disappeared. The 'altered colour' episodes and shutter-like effects were no longer there. However, I still had blurry vision in one eye, and images appeared overlapped, rendering me unable to focus on what I saw. Upon her initial examination, the ophthalmologist confirmed that only one eye seemed to have some sort of vision deficit.

Another worry that lingered in my mind was a condition I had experienced ten years earlier, vitreous detachment in my right eye. This is a condition when the gel-like substance that fills the eye and gives it its round shape, shrinks and detaches from the inner surface of the eye. When I had suffered from vitreous detachment, I experienced seeing little bright dots in my vision field. Basically, I was seeing stars, although not quite like in the cartoons. Then, it began to darken as if a dimmer switch was slowly shutting out the light and turning the room dark, until it became pitch black.

At that time, I was working in the otorhinolaryngology (a.k.a. Ear, Nose, Throat—ENT) clinic of a major urban hospital. Perhaps, I had been peering down the small eyepieces of the otoscope and microscopes doing examinations and procedures all day and my eyes simply could not take the strain any more. I remember resting and taking the patch-paddle for cye-examinations to close one eye at a time as a form of self-assessment. The darkness appeared to have affected only the eye that I used for looking into the otoscope.

The ENT clinic was right next to the ophthalmology clinic. Because I had already seen my last patient for the morning, I walked over next door and related my symptoms to my colleague. Upon examination, the source of my vision problem was traced to vitreous detachment. Since the situation could result in loss of vision, I was given an appointment to have the problem corrected using a laser procedure—sort of using a laser beam to 'glue' the gel substance back to the inner surface where it belonged. After that treatment, I had no further problems with my vision . . . until now. Due to some, albeit remote, similarity of the symptoms, like the shutter-effect that I was experiencing, I wondered whether the vitreous detachment had recurred.

To investigate further, the ophthalmologist decided to examine the insides of the eyes. By doing so, she would be able to inspect the retina more closely.

After the tests were completed, the eye doctor reported that there was nothing physically wrong with my eyes. She further added, 'Whatever the problem is, it seems to be coming from "higher up" and not the eye itself.' I remember being relieved at first because there was nothing wrong with my eyes. Then of course the realization dawned on me that what she had just said simply pointed back to what I had feared—the possibility that I had suffered another stroke.

I walked back to my neurologist's consultation room with a heavy heart because I could anticipate what she was going to say next: 'We have to do an MRI . . . it could be another stroke.' Although I had expected that, I still felt numb when I heard her words. It was another blow and this time it seemed to hurt so much more. Even more than the pain I had experienced when I had had my heart surgery only three months ago.

My heart sank with despair and frustration but all I could manage was to scream in silence. The silent screams of my repressed fear and despair echoed within the deepest reaches of my psyche. How I wished I could let everyone know how I really felt instead of showing that mask of calmness and acceptance.

I knew my husband was devastated, but he too put on a similar façade of the stoic calmness of six months ago. Back then, we had walked into the same room, seen the same doctor and heard that same devastating word—stroke. It must have been just as difficult for my neurologist to convey that message, again. As a doctor, I would have been quite depressed to be in her position.

I felt like I was spiralling uncontrollably into the same cycle that I had gone through when I had my previous strokes. Little did I know at the time that this was going to be an even longer journey, fraught with even more obstacles. Seemingly losing control of the direction that your life is going, and in that helpless way, was a dreadful feeling.

It is probably a feeling that everyone who has ever suffered a serious illness has experienced—a mixture of dread and despair attached to a sense of hopelessness. Of course, one can always argue that the control we have over the direction our lives take is merely an illusion. The individual is never really in control on the path that fate has decreed.

An urgent MRI was arranged for me. Prior to my heart surgery, I had undergone at least three MRIs, and two CT-scans. That's probably more than many people will undergo in a lifetime. In my case, I had those procedures very close to each other. Little did I know then how many more MRIs would be in store for me over a period of a year and a half.

Since I had done the procedure several times previously, I knew what to expect. The imaging process I had been through before took about forty-five minutes to an hour. The first few times it was quite uncomfortable due to the knocking and banging sounds the machine made. But this time around, I do not remember the cacophony of whirrs, bangs and knocks as really bothering me. Perhaps it was because I was too preoccupied with what was happening to me to register the machine's clanking.

I think I may have slept through almost the entire procedure. I only remember that suddenly it was all over. I went straight back to my neurologist's consultation room without trying to peek at the report that was handed to me. When I was diagnosed with the stroke caused by the heart tumour, I had peeked at my MRI report and sort of already knew what the doctor was going to tell me—not that it lessened the shock of her diagnosis in any way. This time, I simply didn't want to know.

'It looks like an infarct. The lesion is at the same spot as your previous strokes,' was how my neurologist quickly got her explanation out of the way.

I was shocked speechless. An infarct was the medical term for dead tissue caused by loss of blood supply (ischemia). A stroke and a heart attack would therefore be referred to as an infarct. For a while, I just heard her talking without properly listening to her actual words or saying anything in return. Perhaps it was the anguish of hearing the stroke diagnosis again.

I admit that I was worried that there could have been some lasting damage from my previous stroke episodes. My worry had been that the damage from those strokes was the cause of my vision problems. But this diagnosis of my having had yet another stroke was an unexpected blow. I had thought that that particular problem would be something that would not bother me for a while and that the heart surgery was successful in resolving the problem. My cardiologist had already repeated an ultrasound imaging of my heart to see if the tumour was still present and it was not.

As a doctor, I was well aware that strokes could occur for other reasons. But I did not seem to be at risk for those other reasons. After that initial shock of being told I had probably had another stroke, I snapped my wandering mind back to attending the matter at hand.

My neurologist's tone and expression seemed to be different from usual as she explained the diagnosis. I felt that she was very careful and guarded in her words as she conveyed to me the radiology findings and how she intended to proceed.

I noticed then that she kept referring to it quite often as 'the lesion', although she had said it was a stroke. My mind became fully alert again.

Was there something which I had missed earlier? Did she mean that there was something else there? Or was she referring to brain scarring from my previous strokes? It seemed the finding was not as straightforward as just yet another stroke. I had been warned that the site of my strokes could become scarred similar to the way wounds can get scarred. This scarring of the brain could lead to other problems such as seizures.

Later, when I actually read the radiologist's report, I understood why my neurologist had repeatedly used the term lesion. The radiologist had actually written in the report the term 'hyperintense lesion'. In other words, he was saying that he saw something 'glowing' in the brain MRI that was not normal, at the same site as the previous stroke. It looked like it was a stroke. I had seen MRIs of strokes and I would agree that it did look like a stroke. But this radiologist had been the same one that reported my previous strokes—so he had compared the new images to the previous images. Just the fact that it appeared at the same site as before was a tell-tale sign that something else might be going on.

3

MRI, Am are I?

A lesion could be any abnormal region in a tissue or organ that is damaged due to injury or disease. A stroke site could of course be described as a lesion. In my case, it was a well-defined, roundish-shaped lesion just sitting there in the left parietal lobe of my brain.

When the MRI images were viewed further, there appeared to be a tail-like protrusion from the main oval shape of the lesion. I could clearly see it on the images when it was pointed out to me. However, the problem was that strokes do not usually occur at the same spot.

During my previous stroke episodes prior to heart surgery, the sites where the strokes happened had always been the same. It was something my neurologists had noticed and pondered on its significance. This does not usually happen, but neither was it dismissed as an impossibility. It was believed that somehow the blood clots had a route or passage that always led them to the same site. But now that the heart-valve tumour was no longer there, what could be causing this new stroke? A new disconcerting question had slowly made its way into consideration—was it even a stroke?

My brain began to crunch away—I started downloading all the information stored in my memory from all the medical training and listed the possible diagnoses that I could think of, matching my symptoms and the MRI finding. I must admit that since I did not specialize in neurology or radiology, there was not much to recall. It was not something I had come across in practice, nor could I remember it from any medical text. I resolved then that I needed to figure out what might be happening to me from the medical literature.

I wanted immediate answers and a clear plan. I refused to accept the uncertainty of my situation. I still believed that my vision problems were my brain's way of repairing or rewiring the damaged area after my previous strokes. The visual signal pathway was somewhere close enough to the infarcted site, so it was always possible that it had been affected by my previous strokes. Unfortunately, that certainty gradually faded away as my neurologist finally narrowed down to the problem of the strokes occurring at the same site, and dismissed it as an unlikely possibility—particularly because I no longer had the heart-valve tumour.

Since there was nothing that could be done at the hospital, I was not warded. The plan my neurologist had drawn up involved my getting referred to another hospital where there were consultant neuro-radiologists in residence. These were basically radiologists who specialized even further in the diagnostic imaging of the brain. The hospital with the neuro-radiologists also had an MRI machine that was able to provide even higher resolution images that could provide a sort of map of the blood vessels in the brain. This would allow the blood vessels leading to the site to be imaged and with that, hopefully, also explain why the site appears 'hyperintense' on my MRIs.

It had been a while since I cried with despair but that night, with the anguish of this new diagnosis and the uncertainty that accompanied it, I couldn't control my tears from flowing again. Knowing that I had something abnormal in my brain was just depressing. For months I had struggled but eventually learned to accept what had happened to me—the strokes, the heart tumour and the open-heart surgery. It was true that I was optimistic throughout my recovery following the surgery. My optimism had probably stemmed from the fact that there was an end in sight. My heart surgery was the means to ending the strokes. Or so I believed.

The enigma of my recurring hyperintense lesion weighed heavily in my mind. At the soonest opportunity I had upon returning home, I searched the web for situations and known cases that could result in recurrent hyperintense spots in MRIs. In hindsight, that was perhaps not a good idea. I had no idea what I was really dealing with, but the searches managed to return a number of possibilities, all of them rather grim. I think not knowing all those possibilities would have made the waiting more bearable and definitely less stressful.

I was far from ready to hear any more shocking news regarding my health. I did not expect to have to go through this again, especially after I had just returned to work after three months of medical leave. Was the promise of being healed merely a pipe dream? Was a return to my former good health merely the unattainable goal of a journey with no ending? Well, all journeys do end, but was this THE ending for me?

It was the start of a new school year. My sons were, in a way, also recovering from the upheaval that my illness had brought into our family. With the new year, we had hoped to start with a clean slate towards a future together as a family again—not with my being hospitalized for days on end. To my family, as it was for me, the heart surgery was a closure, a sort of happy ending.

My two boys had made a colourful painting that perhaps reflected their feelings with the words 'Mama's heart fixed' across what appeared to be a big heart. However, now the story seemed to be replaying itself with new twists in the plot and seemingly new cast members. It was hard just thinking about how they would cope. I did not know how to tell them the news I had received. I did not ever want to see the sadness in their faces that I could still make out etched behind their brave expressions during my previous illness.

A few days later, I received a call from my neurologist. 'I've booked an appointment for you to see the neuro-radiologist next Monday. Please bring all your previous films and reports for him to see,' she told me over the phone.

When the day finally arrived, I waited anxiously outside the radiology clinic with a referral letter from my neurologist and a bag full of my MRI films and reports. I felt guilty that my husband had to be dragged along again. Deep down, I considered my illness and myself a burden to my husband and to my family. I knew that my frustrations with my health issues would sometimes leave me with a short temper. I was easily agitated and annoyed—sometimes snapping responses that I knew were hurtful. I felt that the change in temperament might have stemmed from my own feelings of helplessness, or uselessness even.

After some time waiting, we were finally called in to see the neuro-radiologist. 'I want good news please,' I whispered to myself—a form of perhaps delusional self-assurance that nothing was wrong. But, deep down, I was not sure I believed myself. It wasn't a good feeling—that sense of knowing, of seeing through a lie, a self-deception which you knew to be exactly that. Although the abnormality in my MRI finding was obvious, my doctors were uncertain about what the lesion could possibly be.

After reading the referral letter from my neurologist and discussing my medical history with me, the radiologist calmly studied the previous reports and the series of my MRI images. In addition to his computer screen, the images were also projected on to a clear section of his clinic's wall that doubled as a sort of large screen that was used to guide us through his observations. Shortly after, another radiologist joined us and sat in on the discussion. We listened attentively to every single word said. They did not seem alarmed. That was good, I thought. Or maybe they were just the unflappable types who never got excited. Either way I could not tell. I just took that as a good sign.

The senior neuro-radiologist was doing the talking, 'I cannot conclude anything just yet. There are many possibilities. That lesion could still be an infarct, it could be scar tissue or it may be a slow-growing tumour.' And there it was, the elephant in the room that no one wanted to address trying to hide in the corner of the room—a brain tumour. It had actually been one of the possibilities that my Internet search regarding hyperintense MRIs had turned up.

He continued very carefully, 'However, based on what I saw in those films, the lesion does not exhibit the typical features we usually see on MRI for those conditions. It looks like an infarct but not a typical one. This lesion shows persistent hyperintensity on the T1 images.[1] An infarct does not usually look like that after several months. If it is a tumour, there will be an enhancement seen at the area, but I did not see any. I think it's best that we proceed with another series of imaging to look further at that lesion.'

'What kind of imaging?' I asked him.

'Another MRI—a DTI MRI. We want a more detailed MRI with a few additional studies on that lesion spot,' he explained.

The abbreviation meant nothing to me. I had no idea what a DTI MRI was or what DTI stood for and how it was different from those that I had already undergone. Everything else was a blur.

Sometimes, I wished that my doctors could read my mind and see just how exhausted I was from all the tests. Don't get me wrong. I'm not blaming them for my ordeal. They simply had no answers to give me. As a doctor myself, I know that doctors will make decisions on what they deem best for the patients. Another MRI does not sound like much, it is usually not a painful procedure—boring and cold, yes, but not painful. But to me, another MRI meant that there were still no answers, just

---

[1] T1 simply refers to one of the many types of images in a typical MRI scan.

more questions being asked and more tests to try and answer those questions.

Being given another date for yet another MRI made me acknowledge that perhaps 'the waiting' was the real test for me—that was my fervent hope. Maybe my illness was just a test of my patience and gratitude. Maybe it was all nothing sinister but a mere trial to see if I could appreciate the life that I had been given. I felt that my patience was wearing thin. My doctors seemed to acknowledge that there seemed to be something wrong with me, but no one was sure what it was.

I often reminded myself to hold back from being too aggressive with my enquiries so that I would not intimidate my doctors. I wanted them to have the space to carry out their jobs and treat me without my constant questions. Unfortunately, that was not as easy as it sounds. In this day and age, when information is just literally at your fingertips, I could easily look for information online or ask around in social media. The end results are that you might start asking unnecessary questions and this can easily take you out of the differential diagnosis path that your doctor is already on. I guessed that was the dilemma my doctors were facing as well. They perhaps knew that I was asking similar, if not the same, questions and might have even been on the same differential diagnosis path.

Trying not to question my doctors or second-guess them was something that I had to keep in check. But I was getting desperate for answers. Now, all I knew was that everyone seemed to agree there was something going on that wasn't quite right in my brain—unfortunately no one knew enough to tell me what that something was.

A doctor-cum-patient should understand when to let their more able colleagues carry on with their jobs. In an ill state, you are obviously not able to care for yourself. In such a situation, even the most junior doctor, just out of medical school, may be more capable than you. On the other hand, the treating doctor should not assume that just because the patient is also a doctor, he or she actually understands his or her illnesses and the treatment plan in depth.

I did come across a few doctors who did treat me in such a way. In their defence, they probably felt that they should not patronize a colleague, so they went about their business of implementing the diagnostic or treatment plan as if it were the most obvious thing in the world to do. Perhaps it was and should have been obvious to any doctor—but it probably wasn't to one who was drugged up, had a splitting headache, been getting seizures, barely had the appetite to eat any food and whose mind was elsewhere, most of the time thinking about her family and her uncertain future—in other words, a doctor like me.

At the end of the day, a doctor patient is just that, a patient. They tend to behave like any other patient. Years of medical training might just fly out of the window the moment you set yourself on that hospital bed. I admit to doing silly things such as asking obvious questions that I knew the answer to; but, somehow, the answers sounded safe and reassuring when they came from my doctor. I remember asking my neurologist whether I really, really (throw in a few more reallys) needed a lumbar puncture (to take a sample of the spinal fluid) that she wanted to do on me. I was fully aware that I needed it and what the risks were; but well, doctors can be just as fearful of long needles as any other patient. Somehow, even though the answers she provided were the same as I knew them to be, they sounded much more comforting and definite coming from her.

Perhaps another 'problem' with modern medicine is how large the body of medical knowledge has grown. This knowledge and the practices associated with them are subdivided into the many medical specialties and even sub-specialties.

One easy example is my heart tumour. The term for that particular heart tumour is 'papillary fibroelastoma' or 'giant Lambl's excrescences' (although there is a difference between those two, we'll not go into it here). My cardiologist had written down the two terms knowing that I would have wanted to look it up further. It was a condition specific to the heart, so it was unsurprising that there were many doctors whom I encountered during my illness who had never even heard of it. But that did not mean that they were any less capable in the specific area of their specialization or as a doctor in general. As a matter of fact, a few who I respected felt the term was rather a mouthful and preferred to go with the highly technical reference of 'that thing'—and I did not think any less of them because of it.

The waiting period for yet another MRI had also given me an opportunity to appreciate and reflect on my emotional and physical fragility that I thought I had managed to overcome after the challenging, post- heart-surgery months. I had been blessed with a second chance at life after waking up from heart surgery. My heart had been stopped, fixed and restarted. I felt relieved and was optimistically pushing myself towards a speedy recovery. My family members were perhaps in the same boat. We had managed to sail through a storm together, and we felt that the winds had calmed down for a relatively smoother journey.

Unfortunately, dark clouds were looming over the horizon. In our elation and relief, we had not noticed the ominous signs, or perhaps we did, but were in a state of disbelief that a new storm could gather again so soon. I was lulled into a false sense of security arising from the fact that because the apparent source of my strokes was gone, I was no longer at risk of them, at least not in the short term. Maybe I had forgotten that there was never a guarantee that I would be well ever after.

Life itself is so fragile and vulnerable. With such hindsight, the ability to recognize and appreciate the fragility and transience of life and the awareness to treasure each moment as you live through them are the best gifts life could offer. I took solace that I had to draw on whatever reserves of strength I had to endure patiently and to appreciate this recognition and awareness.

The DTI MRI took longer than the regular MRIs that I had undergone previously because of additional tests and the need to take different types of images. I had looked up DTI MRIs on the Internet when I got home. The DTI actually stood for 'diffusion tensor imaging'. Many of us will probably have no idea what that means, I didn't either. Perhaps the main difference that was obvious to me was the fact that while all the other MRI images were more or less black, white and various shades of greys, the images from the DTI-MRI were an explosion of colour.

I could see colourful, squiggly lines trace out the fibre tracts in the brain. These tracts are basically the nerve fibres that provide the connectivity within the brain. By inspecting these fibre tracts, the radiologist would be able to determine if there was some sort of problem with the transmission of signals within the brain. If such an anomaly were to be detected, it could explain the symptoms I was having with my vision even though there was nothing structurally wrong with my eyes. Imagine having a camera that works but which cannot be connected to the film—the result is that you could click all the images you wanted, but you wouldn't be able to see those captured images.

4

Image of an enigma

I had to wait another week before getting the full report for the DTI-MRI. During that waiting period, I directed my energy towards what I felt was a more important and immediate matter—my full recovery from the heart surgery. Although almost six months had passed, I felt that I had not reached a full recovery. I tried to clear my mind of any worries about the MRI results through drawing and painting. I was grateful that putting colours on to a blank canvas helped to calm me and de-stress me in so many ways.

I had always loved drawing and painting. My busy work schedule did not allow me much time to indulge in this pastime. Occasionally, I did manage to put my ideas on to paper or canvas. Most of the time, it was just doodling or sketching in between patients to while away time at my clinic. While recuperating from heart surgery, I found that I had rather a lot of time on my hands. My physical state did not allow me to do much—but picking up a brush or pen wasn't all that strenuous. I was able to express the feelings and emotions that I could not articulate into words via the abstract imagery that was my artwork.

It was during this time that I also looked back at my journal regarding my heart surgery. In addition to painting and drawing, I had started a manuscript for what I hoped then to be a book. It was something that my husband had encouraged. He felt that my experience could provide a unique perspective that may help others through reading my book. I did find that writing about my heart surgery, my fears and my struggles, were rather therapeutic. Like indulging in art, writing was an outlet for relieving stress. It was also a conduit for me to channel positive energy and thoughts so that what I had gone through could actually benefit others.

Looking through my notes and the in-progress manuscript, I realized how fearful of the future I had been a few months ago due to the state of uncertainty that I was in. The then pending surgery, the following recovery period, coping with the pain, coping with the feeling of insecurity about almost everything in life, then striving to return to a normal routine all compounded itself to a point that I felt getting well was an unachievable goal.

I had reached a point when I thought I was ready to move on and that I had actually reached the finish line of getting well again and returning to work. Unfortunately, an unexpected and uncharted path had appeared in front of me to obscure the previous route I was on. I had initially believed my experience with the strokes and the heart surgery had prepared me to better cope with whatever I might be facing. That belief turned out to be wrong. Perhaps nothing could have prepared me for the experience that I was to go through. At the same time, perhaps everything in my life up to that point—from my upbringing, my medical training, my extended family, my husband, my sons and so many other elements of my life—were all key components that were in place to guide and accompany me through the ordeal of the next year and a half.

With the new symptoms, I started writing again. This routine helped to slowly push the uncertainty of recent events to the back of my mind; they lingered on in the shadows but at least they were not something that I always fretted about. It seemed like the best way to express my feelings and whatever pent-up frustrations I had. I felt that no one understood what I felt the way I wished they would, not even my husband. This was something even my husband agreed on. He had recounted that no one else in the world would know how I felt going through what I was experiencing.

He wanted me to find an outlet so that I wouldn't slowly self-destruct from the inside. Because of this, my husband encouraged my writing and my art as much as he could. Although he was very encouraging, he could also be rather too honest about it. He would look at some of my paintings and say something like, 'I don't get it'; 'It looks scary'; or something just as unflattering.

Paper, pen, my laptop and my phone became my constant companions and the tools of my recovery. That might sound like work to others, but for me, it was therapy. I drew or wrote whenever and wherever I could. I guess in a way it was work because at that time, my full-time job was simply to recover.

My stroke episodes and the heart surgery had made me withdrawn. I didn't want to see people—be it friends or extended family. I didn't want to answer repeated questions of 'How did this happen?' 'How did you get sick?' 'What caused you to get sick?' If I knew the answers to those questions—I would probably have tried very much to not be sick.

Previously, I did not even want to hear the words 'How are you feeling?' or 'Are you well?' I know such words are probably the most common greetings you would offer someone, even if you know they had not been ill. But I did not find any solace or comfort in hearing them even though I knew that they were questions of concern and compassion. But this time round, I slowly opened up to my friends. I no longer minded so much my patients or anyone else asking about my wellbeing.

I felt embarrassed about being ill. It's a strange feeling to have since it wasn't my fault in the first place, but it was a feeling I had nevertheless. The embarrassment gradually lessened and I felt much better psychologically. I could slowly accept that being ill was not my fault. It was fated to be so. Strangely, when I talked to other patients with long-term illnesses, they had said that they too had similar feelings.

Waiting and thinking (and, of course, worrying) about test results has always been hard for me—but I guess this is probably true for almost everyone else too. I had this persistent expectation of wanting to hear my doctors say that all the diagnostic findings were actually normal and that it was all just a false alarm. After what I had been through, I had high hopes that nothing was wrong with me. Maybe I should have ignored the symptoms instead of allowing them to cause me unnecessary worry and distress. I rationalized to myself: I had suffered several stroke episodes, so it wasn't inconceivable that there was some lasting damage with delayed symptoms such as the ones I was experiencing. That was the best that I could have hoped for at that time.

A follow-up appointment was arranged for me to see the consultant neuro-radiologist again. It had been two months since the first MRI when my vision problems started. I had hoped then that this second meeting would be more conclusive. Unfortunately, that was not to be. He told me about having conferred, regarding the imagery of my hyperintense lesion, with other neuro-radiologist colleagues and that they had all drawn a blank. Perhaps if it had been a one-time image and on only one machine, it could have been attributed to a glitch in the equipment. But I had done multiple MRIs on different MRI machines. There was definitely something there.

The image was becoming sort of an enigma. Unable to provide me with a more conclusive answer, he offered his opinion that the lesion is probably 'not something sinister'. Although the neuro-radiologist did not offer more than that, I think the message he was trying to imply was that he did not think the lesion was a cancerous brain tumour. Since no one was able to provide a new diagnosis, the previous diagnosis of infarct (stroke) remained. It was at about this time that the term 'atypical' was added to infarct. The general consensus was that it did look like an infarct, but yet, it wasn't like any other often-seen infarct hence the atypical label. Unfortunately, this atypical label would cause me a good deal of grief later on.

Before I go on, I must make it clear that I did not blame the radiologist for labelling the lesion as an atypical infarct. He had to tread carefully so that I was not misdiagnosed, which in turn could have led to wrong treatments or unnecessarily invasive procedures such as brain surgery. In fact, he followed my case closely even after he had transferred to another hospital. With the evidence he had, there was perhaps nothing much he or anyone else could have done.

Several weeks after the vision problems started, I also began having what seemed to be minor or focal seizures. These mainly involved muscle twitching and the occasional uncontrolled jerking of my limbs. Although these symptoms were considered serious, they did not seem life threatening. To my doctors, it meant that there was still time for them to dig further in order to discover what exactly was ailing me and what the hyperintense MRI spot meant. That unexplained spot on my MRI had cast a shadow that shrouded the path in front of me with darkness and uncertainty.

To this day, I am not able to find the words to describe my disappointment at being told that, after several MRIs and the fancy DTI-MRI, there was still no way forward in terms of treating me except to manage the seizures. This meant taking anti-seizure or anti-epileptic drugs. It also meant more tests and I was also referred to other neurologists for possibly alternative opinions or a conclusive diagnosis. This uncertainty, coupled with all the sinister possibilities playing out in my head, caused me a lot of stress and put a strain on my daily activities. Little did I know then that the worst was yet to come.

PART 2

5

Diseases with cryptic abbreviations

I woke up one morning, not feeling very well and in a state of disorientation. This was about two weeks after the second consultation with the neuro-radiologist. My body felt very light as if I were floating in the air. However, my head felt really heavy with a dull throbbing headache. My already blurry vision seemed even blurrier. I started to see double and strange bursts of colours intermittently. Not wanting to alarm my husband, I pretended nothing was wrong that morning and kept everything to myself. Perhaps I was just tired.

Unfortunately, I started stumbling as I walked away from the bed. My abnormal gait was pronounced enough that I could not hide it and it was therefore quite obvious to my husband that something was not right. My husband quickly caught me as I staggered around, groping the air before me, and held me. As always, he insisted that I get myself checked by the neurologist. At this point, some of you may have noticed that my husband seems to incessantly ask me to see the doctors. But for those who know him, he is far from a hypochondriac. I pondered his suggestion a while as he held me, but then quickly decided against it.

I had just been on a follow-up visit to my neurologist the previous day—I was walking and talking normally then. We even shared some laughs—she could see that I seemed better and even managed some banter. Perhaps she was relieved to see an improvement in my condition. I had also managed to force aside my worries. There was nothing I could do about the MRI images, and since all I could do was wait for other referrals and tests, I decided to focus on what I wanted to achieve next.

As my husband helped me hobble awkwardly back to bed, I felt a deep sense of embarrassment and shame for being sick. Of all the emotions that could have been going through me, I had not really thought that I would be embarrassed by or ashamed of my situation. Yet, that was what I felt. By being ill, I had let myself, my family and my doctors down, again. I felt that I had worked really hard towards a full recovery. I had thought that I had nearly managed to achieve my goal of a full recovery, especially after emerging from the heart surgery feeling strong and alive again. Was all that pain and struggle to heal for nothing? Was the heart surgery the wrong course of treatment to take? Had it all been a mistake?

I was supposed to be well by now. I had been able to overcome whatever obstacles that came my way by being positive and optimistic throughout my recovery from heart surgery and the strokes. But that morning, my resolve and optimism failed me. My legs weakened and buckled, my body ached and the muscles on my face and limbs began to twitch uncontrollably. I could feel and see the involuntary movements but I could not stop them. I felt powerless—it was like being an observer on the sidelines, watching as things went wrong with my body but wholly unable to react. Soon after, I began to experience a severe dizziness—everything around me seemed to be whirling whenever I opened my eyes. My head ached with wave upon wave of what I can only recall as a severe, searing pain.

Ending up in such a state again—not able to walk, my head spinning and unable to think or focus; a burden and a nuisance on those around me—how could I not feel like a failure? How could I not feel ashamed and disappointed? So much effort, time and money had been invested to get me well and yet I seemed to have returned to square one.

Ignoring my initial unwillingness to see the doctor, my husband insisted on bringing me to the hospital. Due to my condition, we went directly to the Accident and Emergency department instead of going through the usual registration process at the specialist clinics. Since I could hardly walk, my husband had requested for a wheelchair. I had also brought along the walking stick I had used when I had had my stroke episodes related to the heart tumour.

At the time, a few weeks had passed since my DTI MRI. Unfortunately, there was still no conclusion as to what the enigmatic intense spot was. Was it a tumour? Or was it really just a stroke? I was getting frustrated with the lack of progress. It wasn't that I blamed the neuro-radiologist for this state of limbo. I perhaps understood the burden that he was bearing. It was not a decision that he wanted to make lightly. It was a decision that he had to get right. If he concluded that it was a tumour, the next most likely course of action would have been surgery. Opening up someone's brain only to discover that it was all a mistake and for nothing, is not something that any doctor will ever want to do. On the other hand, if he had erroneously said that it was a stroke when it was a tumour, that would allow time for the tumour to grow and even spread to a point when it could be too late to do anything about it.

Following the development of my new symptoms and the inconclusiveness of my MRI results, my neurologist asked if I would like to seek the opinion of a senior respected colleague who had extensive experience with epilepsy at another hospital. As I had mentioned, I had been suffering from minor seizures and muscle twitches—which were probably seizures too. In fact, I was initially diagnosed as having a stroke because I seemed to be suffering from seizures. My neurologist was now worried that perhaps the site of my stroke had developed scarring and was now causing me to have these epileptic seizures.

Now, let's get back to the seizures problem. Epilepsy is not one single disease but more of a condition that its sufferers, or epileptics, experience—it is called an epileptic seizure or fit. The cause of these seizures is basically excessive electrical activity in the brain. Another way to look at it is perhaps as a sort of power surge that overwhelms all the normal electrical activity in the brain. Seizures can occur to anyone due to a number of things including brain trauma or even if the blood sugar is too low. But for those who are epileptic, there is a tendency for the seizures to keep occurring and not just as a one-off event.

So there I was, one afternoon in April, to see yet another neurologist, this time, an epilepsy expert. Despite having worked as a doctor in three different hospitals, I don't think I had ever met as many neurologists during the course of my work as I had during my illness. I again related my medical history. It was something that I had probably done more than two dozen times over the past few months. Unfortunately, that particular story kept getting longer with each retelling. Fortunately, her opinion was no different from that of all the other neurologists. From the evidence available, it did seem that I had been suffering from strokes. But the fact that the site was the same for all the episodes was still a mystery. And it was possible that the cause of my epilepsy was the scarring of the stroke site. However, she also had something further to add.

Although it seemed that the source of my strokes was the heart-valve tumour, this neurologist suggested that further investigation should be done to find out whether there was something wrong with my blood vessels as well—a state of the blood vessels being inflamed called vasculitis. She added that it was possible that if I did have vasculitis, it may have evolved separately from all the problems I had suffered, but its presence only served to complicate my case.

My primary neurologist had worried about vasculitis being a possible cause for my strokes. She had even wondered if vasculitis could perhaps be the missing explanation as to why my strokes kept occurring at the same site in the brain and also explain why I might be having strokes again even after the heart-valve tumour had been removed. In fact, she had even requested that I undergo specific tests to investigate for vasculitis.

However, this epilepsy expert now wanted to rule out other possible causes of the epilepsy and possibly even the stroke-

The diseases that the epileptologist (epilepsy expert in case it wasn't obvious) suggested I be tested for featured epileptic seizures among a more complex series of symptoms. MERRF stood for 'myoclonic epilepsy with ragged red fibres' and MELAS was short for 'mitochondrial encephalomyopathy, lactic acidosis and stroke-like episodes'. One feature associated with MERRF is myoclonic epilepsy. *Myo*, like many medical terms is rooted in Greek and Latin and refers to 'muscle'. Myoclonic epilepsy therefore means muscle seizures—these can look like uncontrolled jerky movements of the limbs. MERRF could be diagnosed by taking a sample of muscle tissue. The procedure of taking tissue samples so that they could be examined in detail is called a biopsy. The muscle biopsy of MERRF patients can indicate whether the condition of the muscle tissue is consistent with those sociated with the disease—the presence of what appears to be ragged red muscle fibres under microscopic examination.

MELAS as the name suggests, involves stroke-like episodes. My history of strokes pointed in that direction. My regular neurologist had actually already tested me for MELAS just to ensure that the strokes I had been diagnosed with were not associated with it. Both MELAS and MERRF are very rare diseases and they are lumped together into a category of diseases called mitochondrial diseases. In fact, many doctors, including neurologists, may never come across it in their whole careers. That does not mean that they are not vigilant in ruling out such possibilities.

The problem with mitochondrial diseases is that there is no cure. At least not at the time I am writing this. Being diagnosed with mitochondrial disease was like being given a life sentence—a sentence to a shorter life. The mitochondria are cells that basically function as the body's on-board power generator. It converts the input material—sugar (glucose)—into energy for use by the cells. Defects in the mitochondria will of course mean that the body will have a problem producing energy from food. The genetic defects associated with mitochondrial diseases are inherited from the mother. Both diseases will progressively cause brain degeneration.

In a way, my neurologist tried to reassure me, 'No . . . I don't think it's MELAS or MERRF.' She based this statement on the fact that I had other symptoms and some lack of symptoms that made these diseases unlikely, not just because she wanted to make me feel better. But I fully realized that she needed hard evidence to rule them out. The fact that I was being tested for them meant that the possibility existed. Thinking about the possibility of such a bleak, short future was depressing and demoralizing. It caused me sleepless nights. Compounded by tiredness due to the disturbed sleep/possible seizures episodes, I hardly had any energy or the drive and desire to get through a day. Then things took a turn for the worse.

6

Evolution of symptoms

The 25th of April was a Saturday, one that I will remember for quite some time, if not the rest of my life. We had decided to go on a family outing to take my mind off things. On the way back home, my husband stopped by his office to pick up some documents. It was there that I started to suddenly feel unwell. I felt this overwhelming sense of tiredness and sleepiness.

Seeing this sudden change in me, my husband decided to drop everything and rush home. Upon reaching home, I lay down on my bed and I think I must have fallen asleep immediately (or so I thought). My husband later told me that he had managed to awaken me. While I was still in a groggy state, he had decided to take me to the hospital. He had managed to get in touch with my neurologist who had advised him to bring me to the hospital where she had arranged for me to be admitted. He had already prepared a bag—because of my repeated hospital admissions, a packed bag was something that was more or less on permanent standby.

When I was fully awake, my husband explained what had happened. Almost as soon as I fell asleep, my body had started jerking and I seemed to be gagging and struggling for breath. Unlike the usual jerky movements that involved just my right arm and occasionally other muscles, the convulsions were generalized to my whole body and the episode had also lasted longer.

Ever since my neurologist had suspected that I was having seizures, my husband had been told to time the start of the episodes up to the point when they ended. He related how my whole body was shaking and when he thought he had managed to awaken me, my open eyes remained staring blankly into space and I was unresponsive to his calls. It was obvious to him that I had had a seizure or perhaps several seizures in quick succession.

By the time I was told of all this, my seizures had, of course, stopped. I felt this intense exhaustion, but even so, if the seizures had stopped, I argued, there was no need for me to go to the hospital. My repeated admissions had made me hospital weary. I felt that I could do just as well at home since nobody seemed to know what was wrong with me at the hospital anyway. But it was something on which my husband allowed no debate or discussion. He was taking me to the hospital—period.

The next day, at the hospital, I suffered severe bouts of headaches that confined me mostly to bed (okay, so I was in a hospital, but I did not expect to be so immobile). Worryingly, my generalized seizures had also increased in frequency. They were no longer restricted to when I was asleep at night, but occurred during the day as well. My condition was progressively getting worse. Because I was fitting often, I was placed in the Intensive Care Unit (ICU) to enable round-the-clock observation. It was at the ICU that I spent the next week. To this day, the ICU nurses still recognize me—greeting me with a cheery smile and a polite enquiry about my present state of health whenever I pass them in the corridors or at the cafeteria during my rather numerous follow-up visits.

My headaches and dizziness also resulted in loss of appetite. I just couldn't bring myself to eat anything. I picked at the hospital food, forcing myself to swallow a morsel or two before pushing the tray aside. All that I could really manage to keep down were dried dates washed down with a few sips of water. For the next two weeks, these dates became my staple diet. This situation compounded my state of mental exhaustion with physical weakness. In hindsight—it was perhaps the combination that contributed to my worsening state. Despite knowing that starving myself was detrimental to my condition, I could not force myself to eat any more than a couple of dates at a time because of my rather constantly nauseous state.

Seizures are commonly treated by the drug diazepam (commonly marketed under the name Valium). This particular drug has many medical uses; for seizures in a hospital setting, it is usually administered directly into the veins (intravenously). This was thus the go-to drug intervention whenever I had a seizure. Valium is a sedative, but it also has other side effects, among them is temporary loss of memory. Perhaps because of this, I did not remember much of the details during that time. The gaps in my recollection of the events were filled in by my husband.

The increased frequency of my seizures led my neurologist
to again carry out another EEG and of course yet more tests.
Unlike the previous EEGs, this time, she had decided to do a
more extensive procedure that integrated video recordings of
the fitting episodes. This was the first of perhaps three video-
EEGs that I underwent. Basically, there are tiny metal buttons
(electrodes) attached to your scalp that are connected by wires to
a recording device and computer. An EEG was uncomfortable
enough on its own, but having a video recording taken of you
having seizures took the discomfort to a whole new level.

My previous EEGs had taken approximately an hour from
start to finish. However, since the last EEG had been negative
for any seizure activity, my neurologist decided that this EEG
would run the course of twenty-four hours with the added
intrusion of a video camera hovering on a stand watching over
me. A nurse was dedicated solely for this procedure—she was
to begin the video recording and mark the time of the EEG
recording whenever I was observed to have a seizure. What that
meant was that she had to, more or less, just sit by my bedside
throughout the night until she was relieved the next day. Since
we had nowhere to go and not much to do but more or less
stare at each other, we got to know each other a bit. Having said
that, I was most probably not great company in my rather often
drugged-up state due to the repeated Valium administrations.

Having seen a number of my fits, my husband could tell
when I might have an episode—the tell for my seizures, also
called the aura, were vision problems or an extreme tiredness,
both of which would lead me to fall asleep, soon after which
the seizures would start. One worrying aspect of the seizures
was that they seemed to be evolving with different variations

in addition to the convulsions. In one episode I might be blankly and unresponsively staring with eyes open, some occurrences would involve choking and gagging and other episodes contained combinations of these. However, the one commonality for all the seizures was that each one would start with the twitching of the fingers on my right hand, as if I were picking at the strings of a musical instrument, followed by them clenching, but not quite closed, into a fist. This clenching was followed by tensing of the whole arm and soon after the convulsions would start.

The presentations of my seizures were rather inconsistent; adding to that worry was that they seemed to be going on for longer. When my husband first noticed that I seemed to be having the focal seizures in my sleep, he had timed them to be about three minutes or so. These could already be considered as rather lengthy since, for many epileptics, seizures last only about a minute or less. But at this point in time, I was experiencing longer episodes lasting more than five minutes, some even entering the ten minutes and more territory. The effects of the drugs were another worry. Despite drug intervention to disrupt and stop my seizures using Valium, the seizures just continued as if the doses of Valium had no effect. I slept for most of the day—exhausted and also unable to fend off the drowsiness that the drugs being pumped into me brought about.

Since I was in the ICU during this time, my children were not allowed to visit due to hospital regulations against allowing visitors under the age of twelve into the ICU. My longing for their presence was perhaps assuaged by the fact that my bed had a direct view of the ICU doorway where they could stand and acknowledge me with a sad wave. I would return their gesture with as much cheer as I could muster. I was lucky that during the noon visiting hours, when other visitors had left, the nurse would give a nod to allow my sons in for me to touch and hold them briefly. They were mostly quiet and reserved during these visits.

Seeing my rather unstable state, my husband had opted to not leave the hospital. He had more or less encamped himself outside the ICU in the adjoining visitors' lounge. It was as close as caring for me by my bedside as could be because caregivers were not allowed to accompany patients into the ICU. His constant presence in the lounge had not escaped the notice of my doctors. The cardiologist who had diagnosed me with the heart tumour would often drop by and chat, sometimes about little things that were not related to me.

Perhaps that was a relief for my husband. He related to me how one morning, the cardiologist had addressed him with a serious face, 'The hospital management informed me that they have decided to charge you rent'—before the serious expression broke into a grin. In a way, light moments such as those may have relieved some of the anxiety and stress for him. Nevertheless, if that was a tactful way for my cardiologist to convey to my husband to get some rest at home, it did not work. He only left the hospital with me on the day I was discharged.

My neurologist had discussed with me her plan to transfer me to a hospital that she believed was better equipped and had more neurologists on its staff. She believed that since my condition had not improved and seemed to be taking a turn for the worse, she believed transferring me was the best course of action. I duly agreed and signed off on the decision. This meant being transferred by ambulance for about a thirty-minute drive, maybe it was less. My husband, of course, accompanied me in the ambulance. My neurologist had arranged for the transfer by contacting the receiving neurology team in addition to providing them with a referral letter of my medical history and all my test results. My husband hand-carried folders of all these lab results as well as the MRI and CT-scans films and EEGs in a bag which had gotten rather bulky.

as sixty seizures a day. In comparison, I did feel that I was rather fortunate because it could have been worse. The neurologist that my regular neurologist had contacted to take over my case was on emergency leave because she had to care for an ill child. This resulted in my case being passed over to the on-call neurologist. Unfortunately, the ward rounds seemed to just review my case with no progress. My fits continued.

After two days at this new hospital, I was barely able to walk. When I could, I had this strange gait that no one seemed to be able to explain. My husband described it as a sort of 'drunken' waddling—my knees were bent the way one would keep them if trying to get some balance when feeling unsteady; I would lurch forward, stop, then lurch again, with my arms outstretched in front or flailing at the sides. I cannot remember much of that time. My husband attributed this inability to walk to probable exhaustion and dizziness from all the fits and drugs.

My fits continued.

Before my heart surgery, my regular neurologist had tried to control my seizures using a common epileptic drug called phenytoin. It was discovered that I could develop a severe intolerance to this particular drug. When my seizures began evolving, she had tried a combination of drugs to keep the fits in check. Unfortunately, I showed signs that I was allergic to these new anti-epileptics as well. Later, it was discovered that I could not tolerate most of the available anti-epileptic medication. This meant that the drug I was already on, levetiracetam (who comes up with these drug names?!), was one of the few that could be used for treating my seizures. As a result of this, my stay in the ward was now focused on trying to find the right dosage that would control my seizures. I think it was by day two or maybe three after being transferred that I reached the maximum dosage with almost no effect in controlling my seizures. My morale was perhaps at an all-time low. There seemed to be no end in sight.

My fits continued.

The next part of the story was related to me by my husband—I was either fitting or asleep through almost the whole ordeal. One night, probably about five days after being transferred, I started having a seizure slightly after 8 p.m. As usual, I felt this extreme exhaustion coming on accompanied by a severe headache. I fell asleep and started convulsing. Unfortunately, this particular episode did not stop as usual. It was broken for a while, but while still in the drowsy, post-ictal state, I started to have yet another seizure.

The post-ictal state is the period that follows a seizure.

This particular seizure turned out to be a long series of seizures. I remember nothing about that night. My husband related to me that at times the seizures appeared to taper off and when it looked like I was in the post-ictal state, another seizure would start. At that point of my stay in the hospital, my seizures had a pattern of going on for approximately ten minutes, sometimes slightly more, for each episode. However, on that particular night, they were extending well beyond that.

My seizures had gone on and on with no respite. At that point, my husband was well beyond worried; he said that he had reached a point where he felt helpless and almost frozen with worry at seeing the state I had progressed to. The situation seemed to be getting out of control. The on-call doctor had been summoned. My seizures could not be broken by repeated administrations of Valium. Even after switching to another drug, my seizures persisted. Drug interventions were also limited because I was allergic to most of the available anti-seizure medications used for epileptics.

When it was clear that the seizures could not be broken by drug intervention, the neurologist was called and consulted over the phone. The on-call anaesthesiology team was also informed of my case. If my seizures persisted, an anaesthetist would have to give me a cocktail of drugs that would induce a comatose state—meaning that I would have to go on life support. Unfortunately, being put in such a comatose state meant that even the breathing reflex would stop and the patient would need to resort to mechanical assistance to breathe. Such interventions are carried out in order to force a seizure to break.

The time was some time after 10 p.m. My husband had called home and requested that my sons be brought to the hospital. He had also called my eldest brother to inform my family. Because of the series of fits, the nurses had hooked me up to a pulse oximeter (a device used to measure the level of oxygen saturation in the blood) and a cardiac monitor (to measure the heart's rhythm). At times, my oxygen saturation dropped until the alarm sounded and the cardiac monitor showed that my heart was pumping rapidly and erratically. My husband prepared for the worst. Then my seizures stopped.

My husband related how I could weakly mumble a few words but only seemed partially aware of my surroundings. He managed to see my sons who were at the time ten and eight years old. Simply holding and hugging his sons was therapeutic for him. Being roused and brought to the hospital late at night was perhaps something that left a traumatic imprint on their young minds. To this day, they react worriedly and with slight alarm in their voices whenever I need to go to the hospital even for a routine follow-up.

The adrenaline and state of confusion, or perhaps the traumatic experience that it must have been for my husband, seemed to have blocked some of his memories, becoming blank gaps in time, despite being able to recall other moments with crystal clarity. In a way, those moments would haunt him forever. He simply thought that he was going to lose me that night.

Two of my brothers had also arrived along with some of my husband's cousins, which I think was important for my husband. He had felt so alone and helpless watching me have seizure after seizure. When it became apparent that my seizure was more prolonged than before, my husband also updated my classmates from medical school. I can only imagine how helpless everyone may have felt. The anaesthesiology team had also arrived to assess the situation. They briefed my husband on what they would have to do if my seizures started up again and persisted. Having consulted the neurologist over the phone, it was suggested that they take on a wait and see approach instead of proceeding to intubate and inducing a coma.

Then, my convulsions started again. Since the anaesthesiology team was still there, they allowed some time to see if the episode would break. Seeing that my seizure showed no signs of aborting, the anaesthesiology doctor in-charge made the decision to proceed with putting me into a coma.

My husband was watching from outside the circle of medical personnel that surrounded my bed. He heard the anaesthesiology doctor in charge say, 'We need to intubate.

8

An exhaustion of the body and mind

I had been intubated, put into an induced coma and moved to the ICU. This meant that I was breathing because a machine was mechanically pushing air into my lungs. Using drugs to put me into a coma was able to break my seizures and protect the brain from damage. The next step was to investigate my seizures further. That was the problem with my case, each day seemed to bring forth new questions but, unfortunately, there were no answers to those questions.

Before being brought into the ICU, a CT-scan of my brain was done. This was to provide diagnostic images to see whether I might have had some sort of bleed in the brain that could explain the severe headache I had complained of before going into status epilepticus. The good news was, the images of my brain showed that nothing had changed. The lesion that they had seen before was still there, but nothing new could be detected.

The next step was to investigate the electrical activity in the brain to see evidence of the seizures and whether I was still experiencing any. This meant that I had to do another EEG. A technician was called in to carry out the procedure in the ICU. Not that I was aware of any of this since I was in a deep sleep—if you could really describe a coma as 'sleep'-ing. The good news was that no seizure activity was detected. The ICU nurse assigned to observe me also did not report any visible signs of a seizure. Together with the EEG evidence, this meant that I could be roused from my more than twenty-four hours of beauty sleep.

Waking up from a coma is not exactly the way that it is depicted in the movies. You don't open your eyes to see a blurry face that soon comes into crystal clear focus and voila!—you're awake. For me, it was hours and hours of blurry faces and disembodied voices.

I related to my husband how I sometimes heard familiar voices. When I was able to open my eyes, I could recognize my husband, but other faces were only vaguely familiar. This time, waking up in the ICU was slightly different from my experience after the heart surgery. I felt that I took much longer to get to a state where I could think properly.

There was, however, one burning question in my mind. Where was I? As a doctor, I figured that I was in the ICU. But what was I doing there and how did I get there? I had no recollection of the events that led me to being sent to the ICU. So there I was, in a bit of a daze (well, in a lot of it actually), with no real idea as to where I was and what had happened to me. I cannot recall if someone may have actually tried to tell me during my 'awakening' stage.

Perhaps it was a few hours later that I seemed to be fully awake and aware of my surroundings. Since I had not had any more seizures after arriving in the ICU two days ago, I was returned to the ward. ICU real-estate is very precious, so anyone who does not need to be there will be sent back to the relevant wards. At the ward, my case was reviewed again. The results of all my tests were scrutinized. The fact that my EEGs were negative, including the video EEG which I had done before being transferred, became a major factor for diagnosis.

After going through my results and examining me, the neurologist who had been assigned my case had revised my diagnosis from possibly limbic encephalitis to non-epileptic seizures (NES). Little did I know at that time of the implication of being diagnosed as having NES.

NES, also called non-epileptic attack disorder (NEAD), are seizure events that, as the name suggests, is not due to epilepsy. So, what does that mean? What were causing these seizures? It is believed that the cause for NES is mainly the brain undergoing overwhelming stress. Perhaps one way of thinking about this is by using a computer as an analogy. Imagine if you were to overload your computer by opening up a few hundred windows and apps on your computer all at once—the effect is that the computer will 'hang' or seize up. One way to treat NES is to identify the source of the stress on the brain—which in many cases is some sort of mental stress—and removing it.

That seemed to make some sense to me at that time. Perhaps the sudden onset and treatment of my heart tumour had been stressing my mind and body beyond what I could handle. However, NEAD and NES, used to have another name, and that name was pseudo-seizures. However, the term 'pseudo' in

being used, even if they were small. Small veins meant that the IV injections were rather painful. 'Exercise more, *bagi urat timbul* (exercise more so that the veins will become more prominent),' I was told repeatedly whenever a doctor or a nurse checked my forearm to draw blood. It's not like I've been well and able to hit the gym a lot; but the collapsing and narrow veins were mainly because they had been used so much, not due to lack of exercise. When I had the energy, I would nod as if in agreement, at other times, I would just stare off ahead, intentionally ignoring all around me.

The bruises on my arms were visible evidence of the trauma that I had gone through, but the long-sleeved clothes that I always wore whenever I was out of the house, kept them out of sight. Despite the battered look of my arms, they would likely heal and disappear in a fortnight. The worst of the wounds were deep within me, hidden away from the physical world, invisible to even the most advanced of diagnostic imaging technology—no MRIs or X-rays could see them festering away inside me.

I needed to see and talk to someone who had been there from the start. Yes, I still had seizures. But after the NES diagnosis and my discharge, my state of mind was gathering into clouds of darkness that was perhaps just as ominous as the frequent cellular electrical storms wreaking havoc in my brain. My neurologist was the one who had diagnosed the seizures that came with my stroke. Strangely, that was the only time an EEG had captured signs that I was suffering from seizures. She had been witness to my multiple, daily grand mals (generalized tonic-clonic seizures) and when she could not bring them under control, she had made the decision to refer me to what she thought was a facility that would be able to provide me with better care.

To be honest, despite my exasperation at being diagnosed with NES, I had reached a point where I was even starting to doubt myself. Was I really suffering from seizures? Could I be subconsciously faking them and deluding myself that I was sick? Did the stress of the multiple strokes and heart surgery lead me down this disturbing path? I felt that I needed to see someone who could either tell me that I was actually sick and not going crazy, or at least tell me up-front that I was indeed malingering. I felt that no other person would be more qualified to do so than my neurologist.

A psychiatrist would have probably been the more appropriate medical specialist to deal with my possible malingering and seizure-faking issues, but I wasn't sure I could trust a stranger with such, possibly deep-rooted, issues. In contrast, my neurologist had been there from the start and she was no stranger to all the health problems that I had been having. She had been the one to diagnose that I had seizures. She had been the one to diagnose the stroke episodes. She had been the one who referred me to the cardiologist that led to the discovery of the heart tumour and eventual open-heart surgery. She had also treated me when my seizures started to evolve into generalized convulsions. The way I saw it, if anyone should think I was faking it, she should be the one.

As my neurologist got to her feet upon seeing me, I blurted out a request that I myself thought was strange, 'Can I hug you?'

And she obliged. That was the first time I had hugged a doctor treating me. I do not know if it was inappropriate or if some boundary was crossed. I did not think so then and I do not think so now. In a way, all I needed very badly at the time were not more drugs or tests but just a hug. I myself had, on one previous occasion, received a request from a patient for a hug.

Back then, my patient had come for a hug during my consultation hours—she had been under a lot of stress as her husband, who was also one of my regular patients, had been very ill. She just needed someone to talk to and a hug. I was honoured that she had entrusted her grief and tears to me. I knew it must not have been easy. Such was my life as a doctor in general practice—not everything had to be treated with a drug prescription—sometimes, just compassion and a sympathetic ear were the best medicine that could ever be dispensed.

A simple gesture by someone you trust can make a huge difference. At times, no words can comfort as much as a simple, silent hug. Kind and comforting words were good, but sometimes it's the little simple acts that count and have a big impact. To this day, I find it difficult describing how I felt and what I expected from interactions with others. I did not want the sympathy of others. I wanted them to know that—I was not well, but I was trying to get well, and I did not want to be pitied.

What I wanted was perhaps a mix of understanding and support. I did not want others to take pity on me or pile on platitudes. But this also did not mean that I did not appreciate the visits by friends and family during my illness. I did. At the expense of sounding ungrateful and unkind, I had enough of people telling me to be strong and patient. I didn't have much of a choice, being sick. My Islamic faith meant that I accepted that as pre-ordained, it was fated. I did not question why it had to be me.

In many ways, I tried to avoid social interactions because I was tired of being pitied. I was weary of being consistently asked 'How did this happen?' 'How did I get sick?' On the other hand, I was willing to entertain and, to some extent, explain the type of illness I was going through. It was a very fine line that differentiated being asked how I got sick and what was making me sick. Perhaps many did not even notice the difference because what they were trying to ask seemed like the same thing. But it mattered to me.

I found it very hard to accept questions about how I got sick because they implied that perhaps I should have done more to avoid getting sick, especially since I was a doctor. I knew that those who asked these questions did not have any ill intentions. For many, it was just making conversation. Nevertheless, such questions upset me. I did want to talk about my illness. I wanted to make others aware of such illnesses. But I was also not seeking sympathy. I was not begging for attention.

Since my diagnosis was NES, I was also referred to a psychiatrist after my discharge. I wasn't quite sure what to do about the referral at first. I also remembered my cardiologist suggesting that I see a psychiatrist after my heart surgery because the whole heart-tumour diagnosis, followed by an open-heart surgery could be considered as traumatic events. After much thought, I relented and made an appointment to see the psychiatrist to whom I had been referred. I didn't want to be accused of being in denial and, if I was somehow faking my seizures subconsciously, I wanted to know. Receiving remarks

non-epileptic seizures were not to be equated with pseudo-seizures and that NES were to be considered as seizures that had other origins rather than the uncontrolled electrical activity such as the ones detected by an EEG. I also added that, yes, I was sort of aware that I was considered as someone who was faking my seizures and therefore referred to a psychiatrist.

The psychiatrist did not observe any symptoms that he could conclusively diagnose as depression or anxiety or any other psychiatric disorder. Instead, he was of the opinion that I was perhaps suffering from a sort of adjustment problem. This was not unexpected since my life and routines had turned topsy-turvy with my illness. I remembered sharing with him that I was writing a journal about my illness and that I was seriously considering publishing it as a book, and how I filled the remainder of my time painting and drawing and had also returned to work.

He said that he partly drew his conclusion from the fact that I could find the drive and focus to write a book in addition to trying to live a normal life—those were things that did not seem like the hallmarks of someone suffering from depression. Furthermore, adjustment problems were only to be expected with the upheavals I was facing on my health front; that in turn affected my ability to work and practise in my clinic. But had all these factors snowballed into a critical mass, overwhelming enough to push me into a state that led to pseudo-seizures? Although the psychiatrist confirmed that the NES diagnosis meant that I was suspected of faking seizures, his next words surprised me and gave me hope.

The psychiatrist made it clear to me that he could not rule out pseudo-seizures, but there was clearly something in my brain that no one had been able to satisfactorily explain. Until there was a clinical conclusion that the lesion seen in the MRIs was not the cause for my seizures, he did not think it was possible for him to proceed. He might end up treating something from a psychiatric point of view that ought to have been treated by another medical department. In other words, someone needed to do something about that thing in my brain and officially document it as a fact that the lesion was not the cause for my seizures. Despite not really knowing what the lesion was, he saw a clear abnormality that could easily be the root cause for the seizures.

Even though there seemed to be nothing to be done on the psychiatric front, I still went for the second follow-up session. I had found the first session to be helpful—even if it was just a sop to assuage my fears and reassure myself that despite my own doubts regarding the cause of my seizures, a medical professional was clearly saying that it was premature to merely conclude that they were pseudo-seizures. I was discharged from further follow-ups after that simply because he did not think the sessions would help, at least not until the lesion in the brain had been dealt with. Other than recommending that I attend some sort of talking therapy, according to him, I did not need drugs to manage the state of my mental health, so there was no real need to continue with a psychiatrist at that point in time.

Perhaps in many societies, including the one I live in, there is a certain stigma attached to seeing a psychiatrist. In a way, attending to one's mental health needs is an admission of weakness. One mechanism I used to cope with such perceptions was by simply learning to ignore the negativity of others. Falling sick was not my fault, seeing a psychiatrist did not necessarily mean I had irreversible mental illness, and even if I did, I should not be ashamed of getting help and wanting to be well. That first necessary step is to recognize and acknowledge that there is a problem that needed to be addressed.

It is true that lifestyle choices can influence one's health, but the state of my health was not something that I had had a conscious choice about. I had done my utmost to see every challenge positively. As a Muslim, I had accepted it as fate that my illness would serve a purpose and was only a part of my journey to my final destination. Despite that acceptance, there was a burning determination to get answers. What was causing my seizures? Did my strokes cause some scarring in the brain that are now causing seizures? More importantly, what was that thing in my brain represented by the enigmatic spot in the MRIs? Could I really be suffering from pseudo-seizures? The last was always a possibility—but there were too many unanswered questions about the mystery spot to indiscriminately jump to the conclusion that it was, in fact, NES.

PART 3

10

A different kind of life

To me it was abundantly clear that there was something wrong in my brain, however, what was rather unclear was what this 'something' was. Despite never missing a dose of the only anti-epileptic that I could tolerate, the seizures continued their daily manifestations. Although I felt frustrated with being diagnosed as NES, in retrospect, I believe the resistance of my seizures to medication was probably a big determining factor for the diagnosis as well. As a doctor, I can well understand the need for an orderly explanation of cause and effect. I was suffering seizures; the treatment was, of course, anti-epileptic drugs; as those didn't work, I, therefore, couldn't have been suffering from epileptic seizures—hence it was likely that the seizures were not epileptic.

According to my husband, the worst seizures occurred when I was asleep—these were the ones that would result in my having whole-body convulsions. I was aware and conscious during the uncontrollable twitches and jerks—a type of seizure known as focal seizures or complex partial seizures. I would later learn that complex partial seizures covered quite a wide range of symptoms. In my case, the symptoms included experiencing intense odours such as an overwhelming smell of pungent smoke, sudden onsets of strange burning sensations or numbness in my arms, a splitting, radiating headache triggered by loud noises, vision problems and losing motor control or balance for a few seconds. Smelling the smoke was particularly disconcerting. It was almost like I was standing in front of a smoky bonfire; I could actually physiologically breathe but my brain was telling me that I was suffocating in smoke. Unfortunately, there was no EEG evidence that could validate all my visible seizures or the complex partial ones.

The frequency and duration of my seizures seemed to be increasing. My neurologists had started a new cocktail of anti-epileptic drugs in an attempt to bring the seizures under control. The dosage was increased, and new drugs added. Initially, I responded well, but a few days to a week later, I began to show adverse effects to the new drugs. I developed rashes and itchiness all over my body. I was allergic to one drug after another, so they had to be stopped. Could that be why it was so hard to control my seizures? I did not know. Neither did anyone else.

Having frequent seizures was challenging to say the least. For me, the biggest challenge was the big question mark regarding the cause of the seizures. Yes, there was something in my brain—everyone seemed to be able to see that tiny enigmatic spot in my MRIs; but was it the sole cause of my problems? No one seemed to be able to say so.

The situation worsened up to a point when I could no longer tolerate noisy and crowded places—they made me feel anxious and usually resulted in a debilitating headache. Even tight and enclosed spaces tended to make me feel claustrophobic and anxious—it was not a problem that I had ever had before. The anxiety would lead to a headache which would in turn, quite often, lead to a seizure. The simplest solution was, of course, to avoid public places, large crowds and enclosed, dark, windowless spaces.

In a way, although I had this frustration with not knowing why my seizures were happening, I did not have to suffer the emotional distress and angst that my family had to go through. Whenever I had a seizure, that was it; yes, I would feel exhausted after the episode, but I could remember nothing of it. But for my family, especially my husband, seeing me have a grand mal seizure was especially distressing.

My sons gradually began to understand how our lives had changed because of my illness and the major adjustments we needed to make as a family. They stopped asking why we had to do a particular thing or go to a particular place or could not go to a particular event. Both my sons had seen me having seizures. They had been there during my first episode of a generalized seizure. However, at the time, they were not fully aware of what was happening. They soon understood the unpredictability of the seizures and the restrictions my illness put into our lives as a family.

In a way, this constant uncertainty pervaded our existence and dictated our daily lives. Perhaps it shouldn't have been so. But that was how it became. I suspect the fact that there seemed to be no end in sight to my seizures had affected our morale in some way. I was full of guilt at putting my family through all this. At times, I wondered how it felt to see me having a seizure. It was a question that I never really got any clear answers to. To my family this was perhaps more traumatic than my strokes and heart surgery.

These were episodes that they had to go through every day. I could always see their worried looks peering down at me whenever I was awakened after a seizure. Those expressions became tell-tale signs for me to know that I had just had a seizure and was not merely awakening from a nap. Because of the intractable nature of my seizures, each episode was a hope and a prayer that it would break, and that no further physical damage had occurred. Such was the trauma that my husband and sons went through, the uncertainty of not knowing if an episode would be the last to end it all.

I was almost never allowed to be alone at any time. Since I had no other caregiver, I had to tag along everywhere my husband went. I was frustrated, embarrassed and had all sorts of other uneasy and unpleasant emotions running through me. My illness had robbed me of my independence and individuality. When my husband was at work, I would sit at a side desk in his office. Whenever he had to be out of the office, I would wait in the car or waiting area of wherever his appointments were. It became a delicate balancing act because a new environment could set off my seizures, but yet, I could not be left alone without any support should a seizure happen.

I even went to a number of my husband's lectures and seminars that were open to the public, where it was less awkward for me to be present. I felt embarrassed whenever I passed my husband's work colleagues in the corridors or lobbies. To my mind, perhaps they were judging me or thinking—why is she always here when she doesn't even work here? why doesn't she just get herself a proper job? why doesn't she just stay at home and do the housework? I was also worried about the impression they may have about my husband for always having me around.

I developed this deep frustration and constant exasperation at having to always be invigilated. I might have even felt resentment when I saw other people going about their daily business, going to work, doing the school runs or even grocery shopping. The way my life had evolved to this state made me extremely uncomfortable. Every day became an uphill struggle to have to face people who I felt were judging me.

Which brings us to yet another problem that I had to cope with. Despite being ill and getting these uncontrolled seizures, I looked well. I was able to physically do what most healthy individuals would be able to do. I was even able to practise medicine. Seizures are not a restricting factor for practising medicine and in my case, I was not involved in any surgeries that could put any patients at risk. Having said that, to my knowledge, there are no legal restrictions that prevent even surgeons with epilepsy from practising their specialties. In a way, looking rather healthy and well compounded the problem.

At one point, I was reluctant to continue practising medicine. Was I just lazy and content with depending on my husband all the time? The thought had crossed my mind more than a few times, but it contradicted the other feelings I had with regard to my loss of independence. Perhaps in some way, the uncertainty and intractability of my seizures meant that I was always living in fear of getting one.

I agonized whether I would seize up in front of a patient. Despite all that, I also believed that my illness had, in immeasurable ways, made me a better doctor. Unfortunately, in reality, doctors needed to maintain some level of professional distance and my traumatic experiences at the hospital made me overthink things and persistently worry about my patients. I simply could not switch off.

On the rare days that I went to work, I would go home and still think about the test results of patients, whether a patient had followed my advice to go for a referral, whether a patient had taken his or her medications correctly, whether a wound I had cleaned and stitched up would be properly cared for and heal properly . . . the list simply went on and on. I fretted constantly about whether my patients were correctly diagnosed and whether they were getting the best care. I believe my experience of being trapped in a sort of medical limbo—I was ill, but no one was really able to tell me what the affliction was—gave me the determination to avoid creating the same experience for others.

I had written in my first book about how my heart surgery and strokes became the starting point for post-traumatic growth. I still believe in that. Yes, in a strange way, illness can be a blessing and an unwanted gift that can enrich our lives in unimaginable ways. But it did not mean that everything was A-okay and life was without its struggles because I had simply decided to accept my illness. Far from it, each day would usually bring in new challenges. And each challenge needed to be overcome and resolved. Despite all that, although I am sort of complaining that being unwell took a lot away from me, I was also happy at what it gave me.

Losing my independence and the fact that I sort of needed to be constantly looked after also meant that I spent a lot of time with my husband. In a way, what could have been better than that? To him, my presence gave him peace of mind; the fact that that he could see me meant that he was not constantly worrying about what might be happening to me thus allowing him to just get work done. So, why complain? These were the blessings that we can sometimes overlook in our anger and frustration.

Yes, I was painfully aware of the seeming blissfulness, but yet, I yearned to be free. I wanted to be free not just for me, but for my husband as well, so that he would not constantly worry about me. I wanted him to be free to get on with his work, be free to accept invitations to travel and give talks or conduct whatever business he needed done away from me. I don't believe I ever heard him complain. Maybe from his point of view, to complain, or even think about being free of needing to care for me, meant losing me. Despite my yearning for independence, I cannot imagine how I could have coped without the support system that I had.

Many practising doctors have epilepsy and it does not affect their ability to practise medicine. It is a way of life for many in the general population. Unfortunately for me, the uncontrolled nature of my seizures meant that I had them frequently. Furthermore, I had no control over when I had them. On a good day, I would feel well and be able to work. But on other days, even getting out of a bed seemed like I was climbing a mountain.

Coming to work on some days and being absent more than present is no way to run a medical practice. The patients needed consistency from me. Due to my inability to be there for my patients, I made the difficult decision of selling my practice to focus on my treatment and family. I started to view my life from a different perspective, and I wanted to plan my future life differently.

One step towards regaining my independence was to be able to control, or be rid, of my seizures. In order to do that, their cause(s) needed to be identified. I desperately needed the answer to that question. My future and in a way, my life, depended on it. Unfortunately, at that point in time, my case had reached a standstill—none of the drugs were working, and there was nothing new planned in terms of treatment or further investigations. I felt that I had to push for the answers myself. Simply adopting a wait-and-see approach was not something I could afford.

One working diagnosis about the lesion in my MRI was its being a remnant of my stroke episodes. But everyone agreed that it did not quite have the typical characteristics of what a stroke, or remnants of it, should look like. For one thing, it was continuously detected as hyperintense (glowing), when a normal stroke site would usually go dark after a time.

So the question now is—was it a stroke site or could it be something else? After much deliberation and conference by radiologists, neurologists and neurosurgeons, it was decided that the lesion might possibly be a brain tumour, albeit not a very typical-looking one. It was suggested that the observed lesion might actually be a slow-growing tumour. Due to this change in the opinion of what the mysterious spot in the MRI images may be, my neurologists decided that it was time for my case to be re-evaluated by a neurosurgeon.

11

A glimmer of hope

I found myself in yet another waiting room. This was a different neurosurgeon from the one that I had been referred to while I was warded. I dared not hope very much about what decision was going to be made. In a way, neither my husband nor I had high expectations of any progress. That was how depressing the situation had sunk down to.

We had lost any sense of optimism and hope of any resolution. Despite my push for progress, I was in despair. I fully realized that the lack of progress was not because my case was being mismanaged or due to incompetence. They were simply being cautious; treading with extreme care in order to not subject me to unnecessary procedures or push me into a life-threatening situation when I was perceived to be stable.

The only way to definitively characterize the lesion was by taking a sample of it and inspecting the tissue under a microscope. That meant carrying out an invasive procedure—

in other words, a neurosurgeon would have to go poking around in my brain to extract the tissue sample. My radiologists and neurologists had wanted to spare me this procedure since the lesion did not seem to be life threatening.

And that was perhaps where my thoughts and opinions diverged with theirs—I felt the lesion very much threatened my life—and not just that, it threatened my way of life and my sanity—which in turn summed up to threatening my very existence. I was not really living. I was a mind trapped in a living body over which my brain had lost control. I was a soul in a husk of an existence beholden to an undetermined schedule of seizures.

This running around in search of answers left me exhausted and, in a way, rather demoralized. Despite that, my husband and I had never given up hope, although its glimmer seemed to be fading each day. Being referred to a neurosurgeon again was a step forward. But would progress simply stall yet again after this meeting? I tried to not get my hopes up, but yet, the expectation that I would one day be well again was what held me together and kept me going.

The neurosurgeon had a serious demeanour with a kindly smile. He listened attentively as I related my medical history and would insert questions for clarifications. My husband would also fill in some gaps. I was comfortable with this neurosurgeon. I felt a sense of relief that perhaps this was indeed the way forward. That dimming glimmer of hope began to slightly increase its glow again.

But before considering any surgical option, he wanted to be sure if that particular site was indeed causing my seizures. A plan was outlined that required me to undergo three further procedures—a functional MRI, a PET scan and more video telemetry EEG. It was hoped that these procedures would provide a deeper picture of what was going on with me and also serve as a preparation for surgery, if surgery was needed.

The functional MRI (fMRI), is a procedure that required me to provide responses to specific tasks requested by the radiographer, as opposed to just lying still. In my case, I was given visual stimuli and requested to respond to them. I was also requested to make specific movements such as moving my fingers.

The point of doing all this was to identify which parts of the brain were doing what. This would then provide a map of the brain that the surgeon could use to avoid causing damage that could result in loss of functions such as vision or motor control. The product of this was yet another set of cryptic colourful images. The good news was that there did not appear to be any changes to the lesion. It wasn't growing. But it didn't seem to be going away either.

The second procedure for me to undergo was an extended video telemetry EEG. This was very much like the other EEGs that I had undergone, but with one major difference. Previously, the longest video EEG I had taken lasted approximately twenty-four hours. This one was scheduled to last for three to five days. If I developed seizures and they had gleaned enough data in three days, I could go home; if not, I would have to stay on for five days.

I wanted to be home as soon as possible, but getting lots of seizures did not seem like the best way to win prizes. Extended video EEGs became something that I really disliked. You are basically observed twenty-four hours a day by technicians in different shifts—with probes glued to your head (they had not started using the probes that came with an easy-to-don cap at that time). This meant that, for the entire duration of the test, not only were you observed like a lab rat, but you also had all sorts of wires sticking out of your scalp like some experiment out of a clichéd, sci-fi movie.

The third procedure called a PET scan (positron emission tomography) was something I had never done before. The acronym perhaps helped to make the procedure sound less scary. The PET scan procedure uses a radioactive material referred to as a 'tracer'. Cells that require lots of energy, such as rapidly dividing cancerous tumour cells, would absorb a lot of these tracers. A scan that detects them would then be able to see where large amounts of tracers had accumulated. As a result, if cancerous tumour cells were present somewhere in the body, then this procedure would detect them. I had to undergo this procedure because I had a history of having the heart tumour and because of the possibility that the observed lesion in my brain may also be a tumour. The surgeon wanted to be sure that there were no other tumours, especially ones that could be malignant.

I found the whole process of the PET scan very uncomfortable, especially because I had to drink the radioactive solution that, in my opinion, tasted very bad. Apart from that, the substance was also injected intravenously. When the procedure was completed, I was instructed to drink plenty of water to dilute and flush out the substance.

Hmmm . . . I had gamma radiation emanating from radioactive isotopes inside me—I wonder what my two boys would have thought of that! Maybe, they would probably imagine me turning into the *Incredible Mom*! Before I was allowed home, I was checked to determine that only the minimum allowable residue of the substance remained in my system. And a final repeat of the advice—please drink lots of water.

When all the required tests were done, it was time to review the results and make a decision. The neurosurgeon had intended to use the video EEGs to confirm that the source of my seizures was indeed that lesion. But, of course, as in the previous EEGs before it, there was nothing there. The technicians had reported that they could clearly see I was having some sort of seizure, especially the grand mal ones, all of which were also captured on video; unfortunately, none of the probes detected any anomalies that could be attributed to a seizure occurring. The medical phraseology used was that 'the EEGs did not lateralize to the lesion area'. So that was that. It seemed like I was back at the point where I was before meeting the neurosurgeon. He was probably going to tell me that there was nothing he could do and discharge me from his clinic.

The silver lining was that the PET scan had not shown anything new and unexpected. So, in a way, that was a relief. I had, on numerous occasions, had this fear lingering at the back of my mind that perhaps the heart tumour may not have been benign and had spread to my brain and other parts of my body. *Alhamdulillah*—that was all I could say. (*Alhamdulillah* is an Arabic phrase meaning 'Praise be to God' or more literally, 'Thank God'.)

The neurosurgeon appeared troubled by the results of the EEG. Clear EEG evidence pointing to the brain lesion as the cause of my seizures would have been an indicator to proceed with surgery. But there was no evidence that the seizures were caused by the lesion. For a moment, he sank into deep thought. To me it felt like he was struggling with what decision to make and the words to use to convey that there was nothing more to be done. It felt like several minutes of deafening silence when, in reality, that moment was probably a mere five to ten seconds.

Then he said, 'There are three options that I can give you. The first is to do nothing, just wait and see how things progress. The second is that we take a biopsy of the lesion to find out what it is. And third—we do surgery to remove the lesion.' I will never forget the serious, but cautious, expression on his face when he uttered those words to me.

I was shocked. One second ago, my life was a series of multiple daily seizures with no end in sight. Now, I was actually being given a choice—no, not just one choice, but three options of what could be done about my seizures. Yes, I was definitely surprised that after months of stagnation in terms of diagnosis and treatment, I was offered a different route. But perhaps not as shocked as I was going to be with what I said next.

Spontaneously, as if it were the most obvious thing in the world so why even bother to ask, the words 'I want to have the surgery' vibrated from the confines of my vocal cords into the room. I was surprised at how easily that decision came to me. It was as if the response had been spring loaded, awaiting the right moment to be released.

'Okay. We'll find a date for the surgery,' replied the neurosurgeon, matter-of-factly and continued, 'I want to be clear that the surgery may not cure you, but let's hope for the best and try to get your life back on track. At this point, I cannot say for sure that the lesion is causing your seizures, but it's clearly something that shouldn't be there. So, the best we can try to do for now is to figure out what it is. Since you want to do the surgery, we'll take it out.' At that point, my vague recollection is that he continued on about the risks of the surgery.

As with all surgeries, the worst outcome was, of course, death. But this was brain surgery—so suffering strokes or seizures or the loss of motor functions or sight or the loss of a combination of the functions controlled by the brain, were also possible outcomes, depending on what happened during the surgery itself. Despite knowing all this, I was determined to proceed. The physical and mental exhaustion of suffering the daily seizures was simply too much. It was hard living a life of such predictable unpredictability.

Despite what may seem as a careless decision on my part to proceed with a highly invasive and risky procedure such as brain surgery, I am still like most normal people. And most, probably all, normal people do not want someone poking around in their brain. I definitely did not want anyone to be poking around in my brain. I had weighed the pros and cons and gone over all the possible options available to me. Doing nothing and simply adopting a wait-and-see approach was not a feasible option. It was already the way that I was living. But you might ask, why did I not choose the less invasive biopsy instead of a full brain surgery?

In order to do the biopsy, the neurosurgeon still needed to drill a hole in my skull, and then stick something into my brain to pull out a sample of the lesion. The particular biopsy option that was most probable for me was a procedure called

side twitching. I had noticed it because it seemed an odd and repetitive involuntary movement. I did not make much of it but merely thought it worth mentioning in order to provide as comprehensive a history as possible. Since jerking limbs could signify seizures, an MRI was ordered, which in turn revealed that my wife had suffered what appeared to be a stroke in the left side of the brain.

Since my wife was under the age of forty at the time and did not have any other indications that could have led to a stroke, a deeper investigation was conducted. These led to the discovery of a heart tumour. Due to the strokes my wife had suffered, we were forewarned that she might also suffer from seizures in the future—a possible outcome of brain tissue scarring from the strokes. This was perhaps when my vigil for the seizures began.

From the moment we were first told that the possibility of seizures was in our future, I kept a lookout for them. However, what I was trying to detect was what I thought to be signs of a seizure such as involuntary muscle movements. Approximately four months, perhaps slightly less, passed by with no evidence of seizures, but instead my wife began to have problems with her vision. These problems persisted even after seeing ophthalmologists at two different hospitals. There did not seem to be anything physically wrong with her eyes upon physical examination, therefore no treatment was prescribed other than more tests to further investigate the matter.

Then the twitches started. She would alert me whenever she felt her muscles begin to twitch. At times, when the twitches involved the facial muscles, I could clearly see them happening. It was a new development. Although it was worrying, these episodes occurred when she was fully conscious and quite aware of them. Another new development was some sort of twitching involving her fingers—although these seemed to occur when she was asleep.

Since I had been on the lookout for potential seizures during sleep, I had noticed them. They seemed rather harmless— imagine holding out your hand and having the index finger shake up and down very quickly—that was what it looked like. When we reported them to the neurologist, she noted that they were probably some form of seizures and requested that I make a video recording if possible and also to try and time how long they lasted.

One evening, in April 2015, probably about a month after the twitches started, my wife suddenly complained of an extreme tiredness. We were out of the house at the time, so she requested to be brought home in order to rest. Upon reaching home, she immediately headed to bed and within seconds seemed to be fast asleep. Perhaps only a minute into what seemed to be sleep from exhaustion, the shaking started. Despite being on the lookout for seizures, I was unprepared for the first time that she had generalized convulsions. I can sum up the experience in one word—frightening.

I had undergone work-safety training that included how to respond to incidents of seizures. These periodic training sessions were mandatory to ensure that we were well versed in such procedures. I knew that the responder was required to put the patient into the recovery position. Knowing that my wife could one day have seizures, I had also done a lot of reading to prepare myself. However, reading up on the subject and mental preparation were very different from being drilled into carrying out such responses. So, when the convulsions came, I could only think of holding my wife in my arms in sheer panic—praying for it to end. All I could think of was trying to protect her. I am not even sure if I knew what I wanted to protect her from. This first generalized seizure led to almost three weeks of hospitalization. I have lost count of the number of seizures my wife has had since then. The number of episodes probably ranged from three to five generalized episodes a day, maybe even more. Except for the twitches, which occurred both when she was awake and asleep, the convulsive seizures always occurred after she appeared to have fallen sleep.

Every time I heard my wife say that she was very tired and sleepy, a wave of anxiety and panic would sweep over me. Gradually, I willed myself to not panic so that I could be of some use in caring for her. So, although I could force myself to calmly go about the business of observing and trying to make sure that she did not injure herself during each episode, I was never able to quite rid myself of the anxiety. To this day, a feeling of dread and anxiety fills me, sometimes overwhelmingly, each time my wife says that she is tired and sleepy. Some form of mental conditioning had associated, and perhaps will always associate, those statements to the generalized seizures.

As I mentioned previously, the neurologist had instructed me to time the duration of each episode from when I think they started to when it appeared to have broken. Worryingly, they seemed to be getting longer until they reached a peak duration that lasted more than thirty minutes, after which my wife appeared to be responsive for a minute or so, and then the cycle would start again. During the night that these particular episodes occurred at the hospital, I could only watch helplessly as the minutes turned to hours and the drugs administered to break the seizures had none of their intended effects. I kept vigil to make sure that I was aware when she did get a seizure. I would usually catch up on sleep for an hour or so during lunch time when friends or family were present to watch over her.

During the seizures, all the monitoring equipment connected to my wife at various points seemed to have gone haywire, beeping off some alarm or other. Her heart rate skyrocketed and at times the oxygen saturation in the blood had dangerously low readings. Each time an alarm went off, I would call for help. Unfortunately, there was nothing the medical staff were able to do to remedy the situation. When the seizures seemed broken, and she entered what is known as the post-ictal state, the blood pressure would drop extremely low resulting in the machine again beeping its alarms. By the bedside, all I could helplessly do was hold her hand, talk to her, urge her to fight on, remind her that I was there and say a prayer into her ears, including reciting the *syahadah* for her (the *syahadah* is a declaration of faith in Islam).

I remember the series of seizures starting at some time around 8 p.m. By 10 p.m., there seemed to be no let-up in the pattern. My wife kept on fitting, sometimes for what seemed like more than thirty minutes before the episode was broken, only to restart minutes later. When she was responsive and lucid, I could sense her exhaustion in her eyes and voice. Since the first stroke diagnosis, I had never really given up hope— there always seemed to be a course of treatment to take. That night, hope began to fade quickly for me as the series of seizures entered their second hour.

I made calls to my mother and to my wife's elder brothers. The message was simple enough—please come to the hospital. I wanted my two sons to be close to their mother. I did not want them to be by her bedside in order to spare them the trauma of seeing what their mother was going through, but I had hoped that even the proximity of their presence would give us hope. I wanted to be prepared for any eventuality.

I had experienced, once before, the anguish of seeing a life slowly fade away as I stood along with my family members by my grandmother's bedside. The same anguish was there again this time—a feeling of helplessness as you try to grasp at hope and yet it keeps slipping away. Each break in the cycle brought hope and each start took it away again. I did not know how much longer my wife would have the energy to keep it up.

My sons arrived about thirty or forty minutes after I had made the call. I took them in to see their mother during a lull in between seizures. Their sleepy, young faces were in a confused daze, uncertain why they had been aroused in the dead of night and brought to the hospital all of a sudden to see their mother. They had always visited only during the day, either at lunch time or in the evenings and could probably tell that something was amiss simply because of the timing of this particular visit. Their voices were anxious with a hint of distress.

I had wanted to give my wife and sons a chance to gaze upon each other's beloved faces. I wanted to be prepared and let each have that last moment if it was fated to be so. Soon, my brothers-in-law also arrived. At about the same time, my cousins, who had also been informed by my mother arrived. I was thankful for all their presence. It took away some of the sense of isolation and despair that was gathering inside me.

Seeing their familiar faces was a comfort although, in many ways, the ordeal was mine to weather through alone.

A pair of doctors from the anaesthesiology department / Intensive Care Unit (ICU) had been called into the ward to evaluate my wife's situation. They had arrived during a lull in the seizures, one of the longer intervals that extended for perhaps five minutes or so. During that time, they were able to get some weakened responses from my wife as they briefed us on options. Since the drugs seemed to be ineffective, one alternative was to put my wife into an induced coma—this would hopefully put a stop to the seizures and at the same time protect the brain from damage caused by the incessant and prolonged seizures. The plan was to maintain the comatose state just long enough to stabilize the patient—too long, and there could be negative consequences; too short, and it may have been insufficient to break her cycle of seizures.

The two ICU doctors were at the counter on the phone when my wife started yet another seizure. Seeing this turn of events, they took it as a cue to put my wife into the comatose state that they had briefed me about. There was a flurry of activity as they worked to intravenously administer the drugs. One thing that perhaps I did not fully realize at the time was that the effects of the drug in inducing the coma also affected functions as fundamental as breathing.

Since there was no ventilator machine in the ward, a doctor and a nurse took turns to manually pump air into my wife's lungs using an inflatable bag (technically called a bag valve mask or sometimes ambu bag). I did not doubt that the doctor and the nurse would do their jobs properly, but to think that my wife's breathing depended on two people squeezing a bag alternately continues to send a chill down my spine even to this day.

The state of induced medical coma required the patient to be intubated—meaning that there was now a tube in my wife's mouth going down her throat. The tube served to channel air into her lungs. As I had mentioned, two sets of hands were taking turns to pump air into my wife's lungs. As soon as the whole process was done, they proceeded to transport her for a CT-scan of the head, to investigate her complaints of headaches before the seizures started, and then to the ICU after that.

In the ICU, she would be hooked to an electro-mechanical ventilator and other monitoring equipment. The time was past midnight. I followed behind as the bed was wheeled into the lift to travel downstairs to the imaging department. There were probably five people around the bed with jobs to do and that filled the lift. I had no option but to take the adjacent car.

Upon arriving at the imaging suite level, I noticed that the digital numerals of the floor indicator for the lift carrying my wife did not seem to be moving. My first thought was that they had changed their plans and had gone directly to the ICU instead of for a scan. I immediately made my way to the ICU, only to discover that they were not there. In a panic, I rushed back to the bank of lifts. This time, I noticed an alarm bell clanging away from inside the shaft with my wife's lift. Already in a confused and panicked state, I cannot remember what went through my mind when the realization of what had happened finally registered—the car was stalled—perhaps stuck between floors or perhaps its doors were jammed shut, I had no idea which.

I froze not knowing what to do. The adjacent corridor was deserted due to the time of night. The bell clanged on. Then a short lull, before it began again. I was certain that if the lift had gotten stuck, the medical staff attending to my wife would be able to call for assistance, using the onboard intercom. I had no idea where the security office was to get help. My next thought was to get into another lift car and use its intercom to contact maintenance or security.

The rest of what followed is a blur in my memory. I had lost all sense of time—it appeared to have stood still and yet felt like an eternity had passed—minutes may have passed, or perhaps merely seconds. All of a sudden, the doors to the stalled lift opened—the medical staff inside were calmly attending to my wife just as they had been doing before we were separated. They proceeded to the imaging suite for a CT-scan and after that, the ICU. Somehow the opening of the stalled lift's doors brought me hope and took some of the edge off the direness that I had felt previously.

For over twenty-four hours, my wife was in the ICU in a medical coma. During her heart surgery, I had waited for more than three hours outside the operating theatre. Those hours seemed like mere minutes compared to this time round. Not really knowing what else to do, I kept vigil outside the ICU. I had sent my sons and brothers-in-law home. There was nothing to be gained by their being there in any case, so I thought they might as well head home and get some rest.

As for me, I decided to be close at hand. In the induced comatose state, there was nothing else to be done for my wife but wait. I guess the waiting is always the worst part in situations like this. You're overwhelmed with this feeling of helplessness.

I was kept company by family members for much of the time. Several of my colleagues and my wife's friends also dropped by the ICU to visit. I was perhaps most surprised when my wife's cardiologist dropped by out of the blue to visit as well. It was a gesture I'd appreciated and had not expected.

13

A lifestyle seized

Living with epilepsy brings about many challenges. Although my wife was at one point diagnosed with non-epileptic seizures (NES), there were still the seizure occurrences to contend with. My guess is that it has parallels to what many epileptics and their families go through on a daily basis.

Non-epileptic seizures or non-epileptic attack disorder (NEAD) simply means that the patient has seizures that are not caused by epilepsy, that the seizures are not due to the brain's electrical activity going haywire. The medical literature clearly differentiates NES/NEAD from pseudo-seizures or fake seizures that are of psychological origin. However, a previous definition lumped them all together—if a seizure was not due to epilepsy, then they were not considered real. This rather generalized and older understanding of NES became a rather big problem.

When I first understood that the diagnosis of non-epileptic seizures was mistakenly being understood and implied by some of the medical staff that the seizures were being faked, I felt angry. I was sure the seizures were not faked.

Of course, an observer could easily say that my undivided support and belief in my wife was simply because of that, the fact that she was my spouse, thus making me biased. Yes, it is true that there is an emotional attachment.

But my conviction that my wife was not conscious in the normal sense during the seizures was more experience and evidence based. During the seizure episodes when the fingers and arm muscles on her right arm were locked, the immobility was so strong that it would have been impossible to move them without injuring my wife. This was rather out of character for her. She wasn't unfit, but she wasn't exactly super-strong in that way either. Furthermore, she would not have had the stamina to consciously sustain the muscle locks and convulsions for hours on end. I'm not sure if any normal person would have had the stamina to consciously do so. To me, those were rather tell-tale signs that the seizures were not being faked, even if no EEG evidence could be detected.

I was initially relieved upon being told of the NES diagnosis. I did not fully understand the implications, so when I was told that there was nothing physiological that was causing the seizures, I simply took that as something positive. To me, it meant that there was no need for surgery and I was hopeful that the condition could be treated with drugs. My wife decided that there was no point in continuing to be warded if they thought she was faking her seizures and requested for an at-own-risk discharge.

After being discharged from hospital following the medical coma, our life as a family became a rather jittery existence. The seizures could come at any time—the only warning is that my wife would usually remark feeling extremely tired and wanting to sleep. The onset of sleep signalled the soon-to-begin seizures. From there, it was an agonizing wait, watching the minutes tick away, praying that it would end and that she would wake up as the same person who had gone to sleep.

That was how our lives had ended up. Each day brought the minutes of torment when I would wait out each episode—some lasted over fifteen minutes. Usually, I would ensure that my sons were not present. I would request that they go to another room or be elsewhere. I did not want to burden them with seeing their mother in such a state.

However, there had been a few times when it had been unavoidable and the boys ended up witnessing their mother having seizures. You could see a particular look in their eyes that emanated through their voices—I am not sure how to really describe the look, perhaps one representing an amalgam of fear, anxiety and helplessness. For all I knew, that same look could have been seen in my facial expression too.

Our lives became a cocooned existence of interlocked presence—my wife was almost never left alone. When I needed to return to work, I couldn't figure out an alternative than to bring her along. It wasn't an ideal situation, and I knew that it embarrassed her and even compounded the stress she was already under. I was fortunate that I had a private workspace, so there was minimal contact with anyone else. My work colleagues were also understanding of the situation and tolerated my sudden disappearance to handle an emergency, a sudden trip to the emergency room or the numerous gaps in my work day when I would be accompanying my wife to sessions at the various clinics or some sort of diagnostic procedure.

Living with the seizures also required management of the environment that could trigger any seizures. This meant that we first needed to know if the seizures had any particular trigger and from there take the necessary steps to avoid such triggers. Among the recognized triggers for seizures are flashing lights and sudden loud noises. Stress was also a known factor.

The need to manage the environment in which my wife lived, led to a perhaps odd social existence for us as a family. It also meant that my sons and I bugged her a lot about the state she was in, which in itself was probably quite annoying to her. In unfamiliar surroundings, we would constantly be fussing over whether she was okay and coping or whether she wanted to leave a particular event or place. One example was weddings— some weddings in Malaysia would have loud, blaring music to entertain the guests. On some days, she would be able to cope, but for many such events, we would attend them, meet and greet the hosts, do a quick sit-down, then we would also just as quickly take our leave.

For my wife, there were also less obvious causes, such as noises that might not even register as particularly loud or disturbing to others. For example, the sound of a toilet flushing in the still of the night, or the sound of a motorcycle exhaust piercing the silence of the pre-dawn hours were enough to trigger a seizure. We were constantly learning about new triggers that could set off a seizure.

A life with seizures imposed many restrictions on our daily activities. The days became a constant situational awareness challenge and a never-ending struggle to cope with different and evolving situations. Little evolutions in the environment that were harmless to others may not be as benign to an epileptic. Seizure does seem like an appropriate term. Not only does it seize control of one's body from one's conscious self, but it also has the effect of seizing the sense of normalcy that many of us take for granted as we go about our earthly existence.

14

Brain surgery . . . interrupted

Knowing that I was up for brain surgery cast a shadow over the days leading to it. Since I was suffering almost daily seizures, all I could do was pray and hope that I would actually make it to the surgery itself. Many epileptics suffer frequent seizures. In many cases, the seizures happen and pass. It is when they last rather long that the situation can take a turn for the worse.

The day finally came for me to pack my bags and get admitted to the hospital for surgery. There really wasn't much to prepare and pack—mainly toiletries, and some clothes for the day that I would be discharged. For the rest of my stay, I would be wearing gowns provided by the hospital. My admission was on the 10th of February, two days before the planned surgery. I was very optimistic that the surgery would end well. Although I had literally been through heart-stopping surgery previously, I still found myself thinking as I looked around the room and house whether it would be the last time that I would see it. The two days prior to the surgery consisted of the usual preparations—more history-taking as well as diagnostic tests to make sure that I was fit for surgery.

Surgery day finally arrived. As previously for my heart surgery, I was up bright and early. With the impending surgery occupying almost all my thought processes, getting any sleep was really difficult. I was supposed to have been called down to the operating theatre at 8 a.m. I waited anxiously for the OT to call, all dressed and ready in the OT gown. I was to be the first of two scheduled cases for the neurosurgery team that morning.

Unlike during the heart surgery, when only my husband accompanied me during the last minutes before the operation, this time, both my sons were also there. The three of them looked worried, especially my younger son who was rather quiet and reserved that morning. As the minutes ticked by, past the 8 a.m. scheduled call, I became restless. What could be the hold-up? Yet another nervous glance at the clock revealed the time to be already half past eight and there I was still in the room. The ward nurses had no answers to my questions about the delay. The panic started to kick in again. Had there been a sudden decision to not proceed with the surgery?

I kept eyeing the time as the morning gradually turned into midmorning. Suddenly, the surgeon appeared in my room, 'I'll have to delay your surgery a bit . . .' and then quickly explained an emergency situation that had suddenly arisen, about which I will not go into detail here. He apologized for the delay as he relayed to me his intention to sort out that particular external problem first before he proceeded with the surgery. At least I knew then that the surgery was still on for the morning. The minutes ticked further past the ninth hour mark. It was always the waiting that really got to me, but I could probably bear to wait a few more minutes, or even an hour or two, rather than having to go through several more days of waiting if the operation had to be rescheduled.

I was finally called to the OT at around 9.30 a.m. I could tell that even the nurses seemed relieved that I was finally being called for the surgery. Perhaps my uneasiness had rubbed off on everyone in the ward. My husband and sons walked alongside my bed as we made our journey to the OT. My mother-in-law had already positioned herself outside the OT. Once in the OT reception area, the ward nurses hand over the patient to the OT nurses. All the documentation was again checked. The repetition can sometimes get on one's nerves, but it is how the safety of the patient can be ensured. You don't want something else operated upon when it was some other problem that required surgery.

For me, that handover period was also the last time before the surgery that I got to see my family. After that point, when the OT doors closed, I was on my own. I psyched myself up and tried to draw all the positive energy I could absorb from our hopes as a family while the nurses transferred me from the ward bed to the awaiting OT gurney. This was it. As the doors closed, the sounds of the world outside were replaced by the OT's deliberate lack of unnecessary noise.

I do not remember much of what transpired just before the surgery started. I do remember some chatter and perhaps friendly conversation with the anaesthetist as he went about his business putting in various lines and tubes where they

started some time after 10 a.m. On Fridays, Muslim men attend congregational sermons and prayers at the mosque. In Malaysia, this would be somewhere between 1 and 2 p.m. He recounted how he was just about to sit down for the sermon when his phone started buzzing. Seeing that it was the hospital calling, he walked out to take the call. The caller merely mentioned that the surgeon had requested to see him in the operating theatre waiting room immediately.

He had rushed back to the operating theatre and soon after, the surgeon had met up with him. My husband recalled the serious expression on the surgeon's face as he exited the operating theatre into the waiting room. Seeing the surgeon's demeanour, his heart sank. It was obvious that something had gone dreadfully wrong. The surgeon proceeded to brief my husband about how I had suffered a generalized seizure during the operation.

The neurosurgical team had managed to bring the seizure under control using cold saline and the intravenous administration of an antiepileptic drug. The surgeon also related to my husband the series of events that led to the seizure. As he was approaching the site of the lesion seen in the MRIs, the electrical activity monitoring probes that were put in place in my brain for the operation suddenly started reporting signals to the right hand. The generalized seizure started soon after. The surgeon remarked that it was clear to him that the lesion and the sites close to it were highly epileptogenic. Unfortunately, the seizure had resulted in the brain swelling up—or brain oedema.

At that point, the decision was made to abort the surgery. The swelling meant that the fine mappings used to identify the areas of specific functions from the functional MRI procedure were no longer accurate. Carrying on would have risked possible loss of functions, among them being motor, sensory and visual because their nerve fibres (tracts) were close to the operation site. Furthermore, by then, the surgical view was also obstructed by the swelling.

15

A sense of despair

Even today I cannot find the words to describe my deep disappointment and frustration with the aborted surgery, but there was nothing that could have been done. A seizure while under general anaesthesia probably doesn't happen often, but it can still happen. It had been the right medical decision. I came out of the surgery with no additional deficits that I was aware of, so that by itself was a good thing. All this simply meant that the lesion was still sitting there. My worry was that, having been disturbed, it would now wreak even worse havoc, and with a vengeance.

Outside the operating room, my husband had been told that I would have to undergo another surgery. Although I had the option of not going through another surgery, that was just a Hobson's choice. So that was it. I would have to go through the whole tedious procedure all over again. I had wanted this to be over, but it wasn't . . . yet. I had entered through a door which

I thought was the exit, only to see yet another door loom before me. I had been very optimistic on the morning of the surgery that a possible end to my daily seizures was in sight. But it was not to be. Not yet anyway.

I reminded myself that I ought to be more grateful to have awakened from the surgery as my 'normal' self. Everything seemed to be working. The surgeon had done his best. At this point, some context would probably be useful for me to explain what having a seizure under general anaesthesia meant to my non-epileptic seizures (NES) diagnosis. Although I do not know this for a fact, but being a doctor myself, I had sensed that my surgeon had perhaps taken a risk to his own professional reputation in deciding to proceed with the surgery.

I had after all been diagnosed as having non-epileptic seizures and the EEGs that had attempted to detect the electrical activity signalling a seizure had all been negative. Nevertheless, he had agreed with my decision to go ahead. It was clear that the MRIs were showing some abnormality and compounded with the fact that I was having multiple daily seizures simply meant that something had to be done. He had clearly stated that he could not guarantee that my seizures would end, but he could at least try to remove whatever the abnormal tissue was and hoped that that would bring some kind of resolution. I remember his expression as he looked at us and remarked having daily seizures is not an acceptable way to continue living especially with the lesion excision still left to be explored as an option.

In a way, my having the seizure while under general anaesthesia was validation that the surgery was not a fallacy or a misguided attempt at treating my supposedly non-existent seizures. Furthermore, the fact that the initiation of the seizures was exactly the way my husband had always described them was additional evidence that the lesion was the most likely cause.

Needless to say, the brain is a very complex organ. Unlike many other crucial organs, there is no possibility of getting a replacement or even a temporary, artificial stand-in. The brain is also very individually personalized—there are no two brains that are 'wired' in the same way. The general shape and structure of the brain may be similar and can even be considered the same among different individuals. However, it is the connectivity inside the brain that makes each one unique to its owner. The specific connectivity or 'wiring' that makes each individual brain unique occurs at the cellular and molecular level.

Because of this individual specificity, carrying out surgery on different parts of the brain will have different outcomes for different individuals. Over the years, the accumulated knowledge has enabled the understanding about which general area of the brain carries out what functions. But within this general area, the differences start. The brain is also very resilient in being able to adapt—quite often we hear about lost functions being regained as a result of the brain repairing itself by rewiring connections that may have been damaged or injured.

Neurosurgeons, like all other doctors, must, first and foremost, do no harm. The objective of having brain surgery is therefore to stop further damage or to carry out repairs as a treatment. Although I had never ever participated in a brain surgery, it is with some amount of certainty that I say that the objective of the operation is for the patient to come out better or at least none the worse for it. In other words, a patient with a brain tumour can expect to undergo surgery and have the tumour removed, but not expect to lose vision or motor functions in the process. Unfortunately, even with the greatest care and skill, like all other surgeries, operating on the brain obviously entails risks and at the end of the list of risks is, of course, death. Things can go wrong, sometimes horribly so.

As for myself, of course I was afraid of dying, but death itself was an ending. What perhaps scared me even more was that I would come out of surgery with deficits that would make me dysfunctional. I was terrified of being left as just a husk of muscle, skin and bone that, other than in the physical sense, could not really partake in human society. That was the risk—losing something that was working just fine in the process of trying to rectify something else.

When I finally saw my surgeon in the ward, he told me what had happened during the surgery. It was just as my husband had said. By then, I had become more accepting of the fact that the surgery had not concluded as desired. Despite that, I felt an extreme disappointment at still being saddled with the burden of more seizures and yet another brain surgery.

I did not say much. I knew there was not much to be said. Even the most mundane and routine of surgeries can go wrong, therefore, and with something as complex as brain surgery, the odds are understandably stacked against one.

Before leaving, my surgeon again asked me what sort of pain I was feeling. As a doctor, whenever a patient complains of pain, I ask him or her to describe the pain—whether it was throbbing, sharp, dull, pricking, etc. I sometimes noticed how some patients would struggle to come up with an answer. Until I had undergone heart surgery, I did not know that that simple question could be so difficult to answer. And here I was again, being asked about the pain.

The quick answer was that I was in a lot of pain. The pain in my head was probably everything listed in the textbook. It seemed to be a mixture of everything. As the dulling effects of the anaesthesia and painkillers from the surgery wore off, the pain intensity increased. Unfortunately, the pain was not something that I could really describe. I became irritable when someone asked me about the pain.

Was I feeling pain? Yes. Where did I feel pain? It seemed like I was in pain everywhere. But the surgery was on my head, so was I merely imagining the pain? The head was definitely painful—a semi-circular incision had been made to access the skull, which had in turn been sawn out, then the seizure had caused the brain to swell, the bone was put back and the skin was stapled back in place (I had not known this at first) and a tube was inserted into the wound cavity in order to drain it. Yes, my head was definitely painful.

On the third day after the surgery, a nurse removed the dressing on my head by first removing the staples holding the dressing in place. The staples looked just like the ones you would use to staple sheets of paper together, only bigger and they weren't holding sheets of paper in place—that was for sure. I had originally thought the skin was sutured and not stapled. Of course, it made sense to use staples as these were probably faster to apply than the slow process of suturing the wound back.

After the dressing was removed, the wound was left exposed. The clips were staring at everyone looking at my head, or perhaps it was the other way around. I felt the pain, but I could not imagine the pain my husband and children had to bear whenever they saw the wound on my head. At times, the pain in the mind is just as painful as the physical one.

My husband was never a fan of hospitals—and it was sights such as these that he really dreaded. Yet, he would help me clean the wound each day until it healed. With the large dressing off, the wound drain was also removed and the little hole it left behind was stitched closed. The wound area was healthy, I was told. I did not look at my wound at all while in the hospital.

Despite having had a seizure during the surgery, I was seizure free back in the ward. I attributed that perhaps to the large dose of an anti-epileptic drug used to control the intra-op episode. There was not much else to do in the ward. I started walking around the ward to get my strength back.

In spite of the aborted surgery, I began to feel better and could not wait to go home. I knew fully well that there was still that lesion in my brain, it was most likely a tumour, although, without being able to get a biopsy sample, no one could be sure. I just had to bear the pain following the craniotomy.

In a way, the whole process seemed a bit pointless. I had undergone surgery, but not really had the surgery I needed, and there I was recovering from the aborted surgery in order to face another surgery. Yet, what had happened also renewed my drive and uplifted my spirits in some strange way. Yes, the most likely possibility of a second brain surgery created more anxiety for me. But the episode also relieved me of some self-doubt.

The build-up of uncertainty within me that I may have been sub-consciously faking my seizures thus making my pseudo-seizures diagnosis true had now been removed. Despite not being detectable by the EEG, there was no way I could have faked a seizure under general anaesthesia. This lifted a huge burden off my shoulders.

16

'Mama, will you remember me . . .'

I was discharged on the fifth day following my surgery. The staples, however, had to stay in place longer and would only be removed after about two weeks. Fortunately for me, wearing the hijab (head covering) meant that no one other than the doctors, nurses and my immediate family could tell I had recently had brain surgery.

On our way home from the hospital, I had a craving for pasta, salted egg pasta to be precise. So, despite my scalp being clipped together with thirty or so staples, I persuaded my husband to stop for lunch at a café that we had frequented on previous occasions. My husband, as usual, was apprehensive at the thought of my walking around in a crowded space so soon after brain surgery. But I felt strong enough for it and I could almost taste the pasta as I thought about it. After giving it some careful thought, he must have decided that it was safe enough to do so. Since I was wearing a hijab, no one was able to see my partly shaved scalp with little bits of metal holding what would have been a gaping wound together.

The two of us sitting there looked just like any other normal couple enjoying a quiet lunch. As soon as the much-anticipated pasta was served, my appetite seemed to dissipate into thin air. Despite being ravenous only minutes earlier, I suddenly felt full and nauseated. Still, I forced myself to eat. I did not want my husband to worry and think that bringing me to lunch was a bad idea. My husband had to finish the rest.

Unfortunately, it was to be like that for the next few weeks. I could not enjoy any food. Everything was tasteless. I forced myself to eat, pushing everything down my throat because I knew I needed the energy to recover. My husband would worriedly offer, 'You can eat anything you want, anywhere you want. Just tell me . . .' It was easy when I was well, but the offer did not make any difference at that point. I just did not feel like eating.

We fetched our boys from school that evening. I had promised them that I would come along with my husband if I were to be discharged. The moment they saw me, their faces lit up with smiles (or so it seemed to me). I could sense that they were relieved I was finally home. However, during dinner, I noticed that they were not eating much, picking at their food and eating slowly, not the way they would usually devour their meals.

'I have no appetite, Mama,' my older son said to me. There was nothing that I could really say in response to that. I merely nodded and told them to finish up as much as they could. That went on for a few days. I remembered how happy I was when one night he suddenly announced, 'We are hungry; our appetite is back.' My husband rushed to the kitchen and cooked up something for them, fearful that the moment would pass. We had a small family meal in our bedroom. I will treasure that moment forever. It had been a repeated trauma for my sons, but unlike at the time of my heart surgery, the boys were now perhaps old enough to understand just how painful this experience was for me.

'Can we look at your wound, Mama?' After getting the go-ahead, they carefully examined my head. I had not dared to look at the surgical site myself. Unfortunately, the three of them had to bear looking at my partially shaved head, with the crescent-shaped wound and thirty-eight staples holding the skin together, every day. I could see how much courage it took on their part to even look at the wound. I do not know why they showed an interest this time when they would usually not want to look at such things. My eldest son was even able to describe the wound in a very matter-of-fact manner without showing any sign of fear or disgust. Perhaps by seeing that the wound appeared to be healing was also a form of reassurance for them that all was well.

I could tell that my two sons were coping with a lot emotionally. They had grown so much in the past two years since my heart surgery, yet they still seemed very fragile. With age came a better understanding of what was going on with my health. Perhaps when I was struggling with the strokes and heart surgery, they knew I was hospitalized a lot, but the gravity of the situation may not have registered in their young minds. My younger son was quiet from the day I was admitted for the brain surgery. On the day I got back home, he fell sick with a slight fever. Perhaps the burden had been too much for him to carry. He knew I was sick, but being the younger one, he might not have understood all that was happening as much as his elder brother.

'Mama, will you remember me after your surgery?' he had asked me on the morning of the surgery day. That question brought me back to what his older brother had said to me, to tell the surgeon to press the right button so that I would wake up after my heart surgery. My younger son was about the same age during the brain surgery as the elder one had been at the time of the heart surgery. Honestly, that was my fear too. How do I respond to such a question? Should I promise him something that I could not guarantee? What if things were to go wrong and I did lose my memory? Then his last memory of his mother as he knew her would have been my lying to him.

It was not only my memories that I was afraid of losing but also my other faculties. I had to be realistic; it was my brain that was being operated on. I could leave the operating theatre as a whole different person. Physically I might still look the same, but would I be able to do the same things or know and remember the same things? These were worries that were always present in my mind but were never truly voiced out. It was something that my husband must have thought of as well but had also avoided discussing. My younger son's question really hit me hard. It was out there in the open now. I cannot remember my exact response, but I think I must have stayed silent and simply given him a hug.

Following the seizure during surgery, my anti-epileptic medication was increased to the maximum dosage. I was initially given the drug intravenously and this was subsequently changed to the oral tablets which I had been on previously. Several days after I was home, I noticed that rashes had started to appear on both my arms and legs. Gradually, the rashes increased and also became irritatingly itchy. To me, it looked like some sort of an allergic reaction. As I mentioned before, there were two problems with treating my seizures with drugs—the first one was that the drugs were not really able to control the fits, and the second one being that I was allergic to almost all of the available anti-epileptic drugs except for one.

At the time when those rashes started to appear, I was only on one medication, the anti-epileptic drug called levetiracetam. I had recently finished the course of my dexamethasone tablets, a type of steroid that acts as an anti-inflammatory drug. The dexamethasone was prescribed to reduce any swelling as a result of the surgery, particularly the brain oedema. As I gradually tapered down the dosage and eventually stopped the dexamethasone, I began to show the signs of an allergic reaction.

Since I was not on any other drug at the time, it appeared that I may have developed an adverse reaction or allergy to the only anti-seizure medication I was able to tolerate. It seemed most likely that the allergic reaction had been kept in check by the dexamethasone which, due to its anti-inflammatory effects, is also used to treat allergies. I was advised to lower the dosage back to the one prior to my surgery. True enough, as I reduced the dosage the symptoms gradually diminished. I felt relieved.

The staples were removed about two weeks after the surgery. It was not a pleasant experience, let's just leave it at that. But it was a milestone, another step forward. Although I had some numbness over parts of the surgical site, I could still feel discomfort when the nurse pulled out one staple after another, however, it was bearable enough that I did not cry out in pain. The next challenge was to wash and clean the area. I cried the first time I washed my hair at home. Yes, crying had become a regular theme in my life. It was my way of release. I couldn't put up a strong face all the time. In private, when it was just me, or with my husband, I would just let the tears flow. I would break down at odd times when an unexpected trigger would just cause me to lose control.

You know how when we have a cut, we anticipate the sharp sting when the cut is washed. In a way, that's what it was like. But we're not talking about a small cut here, the wound size when stretched out in a straight line was probably twenty centimetres long if not more—I didn't quite take a ruler out to measure it of course. As my husband started to clean the surgical wound, I awaited the dreaded stinging pain that would come. I was terrified that the whole process would cause me severe pain. The fear had fogged my mind and even a gentle touch to the area would startle me. As it turned out, washing the area was not as painful as I had expected. Yes, it was still tender, but after two weeks, the wound was closed and had started to heal well and thus not as painful as I had anticipated.

I had never wanted to look at my wound and would often ask my husband what it looked like. I had also never asked my doctors for details about the process of opening the skull. I do not know whether other patients enquired about such specifics or preferred to not know. Despite that, I bombarded my husband with numerous questions about the surgery that he had no answers for. 'You should ask the doctor yourself,' he would tell me every time.

Caring for any surgical wound is a crucial aspect in recovery. The wound(s) needed to be cleaned and kept clean and dry. My husband had to inspect the area closely every day because I could not feel anything on the scalp in that area. It was just numb, almost as if that piece were missing. I did have headaches, but these were from the inside and not pain on the skin. Maybe the nerve endings had been severed when the surgeon made the incision to reach the skull, hence resulting in the strange sensation I felt.

My husband would also repeatedly remind me to be careful, especially whenever I sat down with my children or when I began to scratch my head. Even merely sitting down with my two boisterous boys could be dangerous simply because they could suddenly jump up and bump into me. Scratching the wound site open was also a possibility since I was not able to feel the pain that would otherwise prevent me from injuring myself. The thought of having a 'cracked' skull was also rather disturbing. I would push it to the back of my mind, but at some point, it would slowly creep in again to remind me of its presence and how fragile it all was.

Having one's skull sawn open is a traumatic experience, even if you were unconscious throughout the process. I still shudder to think about it. Being asleep during the whole process does help a bit, thank goodness for anaesthesia. But that does not in any way diminish the actual physical trauma. I ended up having a constant headache that was at its worst in the mornings while I was in the ward. The throbbing ache would jolt me awake and I would let the tears flow freely as I tried to bear the wave upon wave of pain. The headaches never really went away. Over time, their intensity decreased, but they remain to this day; at that time though, on certain days, they would flare up and as a result I would end up not doing much except sleep it off.

While we're on the topic of opening up skulls under anaesthesia, I thought I might just mention that there are actually what are called 'awake brain surgeries'. During such operations, the patient remains awake in order for the surgeon to test for responses and identify functions associated with the parts of the brain being worked on. This obviously allows the surgeon to avoid those regions. An awake brain surgery seems like 'insurance' in a way that would have allayed my fears of losing my faculties and memories. Nevertheless, I am not sure I would have agreed to do it in such a way had I been given the option. The surgery was probably traumatic enough without me being aware of what was going on throughout the whole process.

17

Of little triumphs and personal victories

Several days after being discharged, I noticed some sensory deficits that caused me to have a sort of an emotional breakdown. I realized that my sense of smell and taste was altered although not quite lost altogether. The aroma of coffee or the scent of detergent seemed so different that, at first, I thought they were new smells. The situation with food was also similar—everything tasted rather flat. Was the surgery the cause of it all? Was there indeed some damage that had gone unnoticed? My surgeon told me not to worry and that it was probably a temporary effect which should only be investigated further if it persisted. But for how long did I have to bear with it and wait it out? Unfortunately, that was an answer that no one could provide.

A week after the surgery, my husband had to be back at work. It meant that I had to once again tag along to the office. This time around, I was clueless about what to do at the office.

Before the surgery, I had occupied myself with writing what would eventually be published as the book on my heart surgery. But this time, the manuscript had already been completed and I could not focus on what I intended to do next.

I decided that since writing had been so therapeutic for me, I should perhaps revert to it. However, I could not seem to find the right words to put down. On most days, I could only stare with frustration at a blank screen. When I did manage to write something down, it seemed more like incoherent rambling. When I thought I had an idea to run through, my mind would just as quickly turn blank again. This simply served to increase my rising sense of frustration and despair.

Since the writing was not quite working out, I thought I could focus my energy on drawing and painting. Alas, it turned out to be no different from my attempts at writing. Now instead of a blank screen, I would stare at the blank art paper. It almost seemed like the clean whiteness was taunting me, as if saying, 'go on, see if you can actually do anything.' My hands would tremble and tears would well up as my pent-up frustrations sought a way out.

I couldn't fathom what was happening. Had some part of my brain been affected by the surgery that we had not noticed? Or was it merely the stress that I had been through? I could understand and even read medical literature quite fine. I was able to think of ideas about what to write or paint, but my thoughts and ideas weren't getting translated into writing or art. These mental blocks simply made me very irritable.

Even helping my boys with their homework proved more difficult than I had anticipated. I was easily agitated and would quickly lose my patience over even minor things like a missing punctuation mark or a careless arithmetic error. On some days, a virtual wall seemed to be blocking my brain from processing anything and I would just stare uncomprehendingly at whatever it was the boys were showing me. I tried not to vent my frustration at the boys, but at times, it would all just come bursting out. I could see that the boys were worried. Perhaps in their young minds, they felt that they were unnecessarily stressing me out. This situation went on for a few weeks before returning to normal, or whatever can be called 'close to normal' is given my condition. The most likely cause of my problems was the after effects of the surgery and anaesthesia.

Despite the surgery having not panned out as expected, I was still lucky to have woken up from it almost entirely unscathed. Things were slowly reverting to normal. The euphoria of having survived the surgery made me forget other things. However, that euphoria was sometimes cancelled out by the fact that the surgery had failed. My emotions went through a roller-coaster ride of ups and downs—a feeling of gratitude that had me up in the clouds could just as quickly send me crashing down as I remembered that I would have to go through another surgery again.

I started questioning whether it had all been worth it. Had I made the right choice in opting for surgery instead of waiting and perhaps just doing a biopsy? The pain and the feeling of despair was compounded when my mind would wander towards thoughts about the impending second surgery. If I had chosen not to do any surgery, then I would not have been in this situation and would not need a second surgery. It was a constant struggle within.

For a biopsy, the surgeon would probably have accessed the lesion through a hole in the skull. Disturbing the lesion in such a way would have caused the same seizure but with maybe even worse outcomes. Doing nothing on the other hand would have meant letting the seizures go on and on—that did not seem like much of a life either.

I cannot really describe the pain I felt. The pain from the surgical wound itself was bearable and felt like the big cut that it was. What really disturbed me was the constant throbbing headache. I would be jolted awake in the pre-dawn hours because the headache made my eyes feel like they were about to pop out of their sockets. I comforted myself by saying that the pain was temporary—I had just had brain surgery after all, obviously my head would hurt, what else should I have expected? I did not know whether the pain I felt was normal or something that I should worry about. Even worse, was I just imagining all the pain when there was really none? When I am asked about whether I felt any pain, I would be at a loss as to what response I should give.

Muslims believe that pain and illness cleanse the soul of sins, thus I could accept the illness and pain as part of a journey to absolve sins and past wrongdoings. I had faith that it was fated. But it did not mean that Muslims were not allowed to look for means to ease the pain or seek treatment for illness. On the contrary, seeking treatment is ordained, but the ultimate outcomes must be accepted. I found that although sleeping and bedrest helped with my convalescence, the longer I stayed in bed the worse my pain became. I resolved to ignore the pain and pushed myself to get moving—walking outside, going out for groceries and running errands somehow eased the pain a bit, or maybe the activities created just enough of a distraction from the pain.

Since writing and painting were not working out for me after the brain surgery, I turned to baking. Following a recipe provided me with some form of focus. I had never ever really baked anything in all my life, but I found that seeing the dough rise and turn a rich brown colour in the warm glow of the oven was therapeutic and pleasing. The ding of the oven timer signalled a sort of climactic end to the built-up expectation that had been stoked by the aroma wafting from the kitchen and permeating the house. This crescendo of anticipation made even the plainest of home-made breads pleasurable and a delight.

Baking also meant that I had to be on my feet, a truly enjoyable feeling when you've spent so much time in bed. It made me feel well. Lying in bed or just sitting around not doing anything only made one feel rather ill. I could stand for hours in the kitchen. I had never really liked baking before. But now, I could appreciate the deliberate physical movements of measuring the ingredients, mixing and folding them together before finally preparing them for the oven.

I remember accidently burning my late father's cake in the oven, many years ago. Since then, I had always considered myself rather lousy in the kitchen. My father was very good at baking cakes and cookies. I was rather good at finishing them all. I enjoyed eating more than spending time preparing the food. Perhaps that wasn't quite a conventional father-daughter relationship. It should probably have been me, the daughter, doing the cooking for my father. Then again, he probably didn't trust me with the oven or stove after the burnt-cake incident, so perhaps it was all for the best.

About two weeks after the aborted surgery, the incision site started to throb with pain. I ran my finger along the painful region trying to make sense of what it was. My finger came away wet with splotches of blood. This caught me by surprise as I had thought that the wound had healed, or at least, had been healing well. I wiped the same area again with a tissue paper to double check. Yes, there appeared to be some sort of bloody discharge from the incision site.

This development meant that I would have to go to the hospital to have the wound checked. At the hospital, the discharge site on my scalp was explored and cleaned. There appeared to be infection in a small area caused by the suture being exposed. Even that little bit of infection could potentially flare up, so I had to be admitted for IV antibiotics and daily wound dressing. At this point, I had perhaps reached a new low. I felt down and depressed. I was suffering from seizures, had had brain surgery in the hope of treating them, but the surgery had to be aborted due to a seizure and now it seemed yet something else was going wrong.

Another admission meant that I had to be away from my children again. But there was no choice; I needed to take the IV antibiotics over a few days in order to control the infection and prevent it from spreading. I started feeling sorry for myself again; my medical problems just seemed never ending. It was during my brooding that my husband, who had been working on his laptop in a corner of the room, broke my reverie as he called my attention to some emails I had sent out a few days ago.

I had finished writing the manuscript for my first book, *The Doctor is Sick,* and I had emailed several publishers using the addresses that I found on their websites. Days had gone by without any reply. I had given up hope that any of them would be interested in the book. That morning an email had come in.

The email read:

Dear Idayu,

Thank you for submitting your manuscript to my colleague, John. (Name has been changed for privacy.)

After careful evaluation, we think this book has got potential, and we would like to develop it into a new series that we are starting.

However, the main thing that I want to establish today is whether you are prepared for your manuscript to be edited. It's also a bit long so we might have to cut out some stuff, especially if there are things that are too detailed or not so relevant or interesting for the general reader.

We will only take it on if you are willing to have the manuscript edited. Thus, I would like to hear your thoughts on this before I introduce you to our content editor as well as offering you a publishing contract.

I must have blinked quite a few times as I read the email over and over again. What did it mean? Sure it was plain English. It almost seemed to be saying that a big-name, Malaysian publisher had agreed to publish my book. Was it real? Given how down I felt at that point, even trying to fathom and digest the meaning of the good news was hard. What did it mean by '*We will only take it on if you are willing to have the manuscript edited.*'? Are they or aren't they accepting it?

The language seemed clear enough, the book would be accepted for publication as long as I would allow for the manuscript to be edited. To me, accepting the book for publication subject to it being edited was not even a condition. I was fully aware of my shortcomings as a writer, so having someone actually edit the book was also an unexpected boon. So there it was—someone wanted to edit and publish the book. It all seemed too good to be true. That was the state of my mind then. I didn't even want to believe something good could be happening to me.

It was a wonderful feeling, even more so because when I had received the unexpected good news, I was tethered to an antibiotics infusion. I felt great. Somehow the gloom and bleakness of the past few days evaporated with the news—the reality of my book getting published was now a step closer. There I was, sitting on the hospital bed replying to the email with a big smile on my face.

> Dear Jane, (Name has been changed for privacy.)
>
> I'd be happy to have the manuscript edited. As a matter of fact, I actually do want it professionally edited since I am not a professional writer. I also realize that I may have overindulged myself in some of the technical aspects and it may not be comprehensible to a more general audience.
>
> I am also open to changing the title of the book. I only came up with that title since I could not think of anything else.

After a few emails, the publishing contract arrived by courier. To say that I was excited about it all is an understatement. It was a publishing contract and it had MY name on it. It was not something I had imagined would ever be a reality. Deep down I had thought that it was quite delusional of me to even try to get a book published. Nevertheless, my husband was optimistic about the whole idea and had pushed me to write and finish it. The euphoria of having the book accepted for publication drew me away from the dark path that I was headed towards—a sinister route that might have even led to some form of depression.

When one is recovering from an illness sometimes one wants to prove to oneself how well the recovery is going. I had never been fond of running and I couldn't bring myself to run just for the sake of running. So, I was perhaps as surprised as my husband, if not more so, when I told him that I had seen an advertisement for a running event organized by the *Institut Jantung Negara* (IJN—National Heart Institute) and that I wanted to register and run at the event.

IJN was where I had undergone the surgery to remove the heart-valve tumour. There were two distances for the *Run for Your Heart* event—5 km and 10 km. I signed up the whole family for the 5 km distance. I was ambitious in wanting to do the run, but I was realistic enough to know that 10 kms was probably beyond my reach. I wanted to prove to myself that, despite what I was going through, I could overcome this very physical of challenges. I was motivated in not wanting my children to constantly worry about their mother being ill all the time. This was my way of showing that I had recovered from my surgery and was, sort of, well.

Despite my husband being fond of running, I could tell that he was not very pleased about it at first and was worried that I was subjecting myself unnecessarily to a strenuous physical activity especially since it had only been about two months after my aborted brain surgery. Despite his initial apprehension, he decided that if anything was to be a factor against me running, it would have been the heart surgery and almost two years had passed without any medical problems arising as a specific complication of that particular operation.

I did not really train for the run. In hindsight, that was definitely not a good approach to the whole thing. All I did as preparation was some walking to get myself used to covering some distance on my feet, but I doubt that I had ever actually covered a full 5 km in one go. In a way, maybe I wasn't even sure that I would go through with it. The morning of the run finally came. The event was held at the National Botanical Gardens in Shah Alam, Malaysia.

Also at the run was another friend from my high school who was a few years my senior and who also happened to be a doctor who had suffered a sudden illness. At that time, I had only been back in contact with her for a short while after having lost touch for years. In a way, her story had some similarities to mine. This shared experience was what got us together again after so many years. She had taken up running as a challenge to aid her recovery too.

The first few minutes of the run were rather easy and relaxing. My husband and two sons were of course there, running (and walking) by my side. It was early in the morning and the trail was shaded by dense foliage; some parts were still quite misty, yet to be cleared by the heat of the morning sun. From the starting line, the trail inclined very gradually that the physical exertion to ascend it was hardly noticeable to me.

Then came the hills. These were sharper inclines that required more effort. Then came another, and yet another.

I was beginning to doubt and question myself. Why did I foolishly sign up for this? Could I be doing myself more harm than good? What did I really want to prove? Whom did I have to prove anything to? I was starting to panic a little as doubts about whether I had the physical strength and stamina to complete the run crept in. I must admit, hills were not something I had factored in when I signed up. My mind had envisioned a smooth, and more or less, flat 5 km. I had thought that the distance itself would be the challenge. Despite the sudden apprehension, I dug up the resolve to finish and take each hill as they came.

Due to the terrain and narrow trails in the park, the quickest aid that could reach a stricken runner was marshals on motorcycles. I told myself that I had better get through because no help would come to get me out (which was probably not true). The hills also made me worry about my sons. Perhaps my ambition to complete this challenge for myself was putting them through undue physical stress—they were ten and eight at the time and had never really done a physical activity that demanded the stamina required for a 5 km run. I actually asked them several times whether they would be able to continue. Both had answered that they wanted to continue and finish. Seeing their flushed but determined faces further added to my own resolve.

The 2 km marker came and was passed. Each marker somehow extracted energy I did not know I had left. I was no longer even running at this point. Then the 4 km came and was passed. And then there it was, the banner that read 'FINISH' strung across two poles. We purposefully strode across the line marking our achievement for that day. The ribbon strung across it had long been snapped by the race winner. Even so, in my mind, I pictured my crossing of the finish line accompanied by the triumphant musical score from *Chariots of Fire,* not the gaspy, exhausted sounds of relief that were the reality.

The pride and joy in my sons' faces remains a priceless image that is forever etched in my memory. I realized then that the triumph was something that they needed as much as I did. They had gone through and were still going through a very traumatic period in their lives. They needed a win. Accomplishing something that was out of the ordinary for our everyday lives can be a great boost. Five kilometres is not a lot. But for us, that day, it might as well have been a full marathon.

The day after the run, Monday, the 11th of April, was the day for my post-surgery MRI. The images from this session would tell if there was any residual damage, such as clots from the surgery, and also provide an insight into the current state of the tumour. The two-month gap was probably given in order to allow the wound and the brain to heal before taking another look at what changes may have occurred as a result of the aborted surgery. I secretly hoped that the tumour had miraculously disappeared by then and that this next MRI would be clear with nothing more to be done than to fully heal.

Of course, being a doctor, I couldn't quite admit to such wishful thinking. But sometimes, one needed to cling to bits and pieces of hope, it was like having knots to hold on to as you climb up a rope, pull by agonizing pull. As one hope dissipated, I reached out for another, and another, until the end. Unfortunately, the MRI simply showed what had been expected—everything looked just about the same. In other words, I still needed to undergo another surgery.

My appointment with the neurosurgeon came a few days after the MRI. I was nervous and worried. I did not like the idea of another surgery—but then again, what sane person would relish such an ordeal? Unfortunately, the moment my eyes saw the MRI images as the surgeon was going through them with me, I knew that surgery was still the best option. Despite that, I asked for some time to think it through. That pause made me feel that I was not foolishly rushing into the possibility of yet another aborted surgery. At my next neurosurgery appointment, the surgery date was set for Wednesday, the 10th of August.

PART 4

18

Brain surgery 2.0

I did not put much thought into the impending second surgery. In fact, I was calmer this time compared to the days leading up to the first craniotomy. Was it because I had been through this before? I could not tell. It had been six months since the first brain surgery.

However, the fear that this surgery could also turn out like before was constantly at the back of my mind. I kept reassuring myself that the surgeons now knew better in order to prevent what had unexpectedly happened the last time. But despite all that, I was still a doctor and I knew that it was still possible for me to again have a seizure during the surgery. Such an occurrence would likely result in the operation being abandoned a second time.

Before the first surgery, it felt like I had travelled for miles and miles through the darkness of what seemed to be an endless tunnel, then suddenly, I could see a glimmer of light shining through. As I approached that exit with the beams of light merging and getting brighter, I was suddenly pushed back to the beginning and the darkness had again settled around me. There was an exhaustion in my mind, a tiredness in my limbs and a heaviness in my heart.

I felt that I could not physically walk through that darkness again, now uncertain if that light was even still there. It felt too distant and unachievable. Was that light really an exit or a mere illusion to tantalize me with hope? It was a dream that I had once dared to envision of my reaching the exit, but now, I was afraid of embarking on the journey again or of even dreaming about that possibility. What if that light was like a star, shining bright with hope, but millions of unreachable light years away?

However, the tireless and enduring support from my husband, family, friends and my doctors especially, pulled me through the recovery. I realized that no one had absolute control over what had happened. In a way, I was saved that day when my surgeon made the decision to not proceed. Looking back, the fall-out could have been so much worse, but it hadn't come to that and I had to be grateful that I went home as the same person before the surgery, neurologically intact. The wound would heal and the pain would gradually and eventually disappear.

The second surgery was planned for after the Eid-ul-fitri holiday, also called Hari Raya Aidilfitri or simply Raya in Malaysia. This holiday marks the Muslim Eid festival that follows one month of fasting during the Hijrah calendar month of Ramadhan. My surgeon had given me a choice of having the surgery during Ramadhan, or after the Eid holidays. I had chosen the latter. I told my surgeon that I wished to celebrate Ramadhan and Raya first.

I didn't know if this was going to be my last Ramadhan and Eid, so I wanted my memories or rather the memories etched in the minds of my family, especially my sons and husband, to be fond memories of togetherness. I did not want to spend this period in the hospital. I wanted to be home with my family. Visits to the hospital during the Ramadhan and Eid period is not the legacy I wanted to leave behind for my loved ones as their last memories of me.

Admission day for the second surgery had arrived. The usual clerking and pre-op preparations got underway as usual. I related my case history or answered questions when asked. But I had none of my own. I was no longer paying that much attention to what was going on around me. My focus was on what lay ahead. A day prior to the surgery, one of the surgeons shaved the parts of my head that would be the site of the surgery. Once the area was clear of hair, she proceeded to put markers or points for the monitoring system that would be used during the surgery.

There's not much that I can say about the time leading up to the day of the operation. Unlike the first surgery, I was called to the operating theatre at more or less the scheduled time. I remember taking a few wefies with my sons and husband. I guess we could all feel some sort of apprehension deep within us. Fearful thoughts that everyone kept to themselves even though the smiles broke the surface for the photos. As with my previous surgeries, the ritual just outside the OT door was repeated. We would say our quiet goodbyes, hoping that we would soon be reunited. Once inside, I would recite the declaration of faith—the syahadah. The deep sleep of anaesthesia would soon follow.

I filled my days with regret at having made the decision to undergo the surgery. But for this second craniotomy, I eagerly participated in every step that would lead to my recovery. I kept my silence and tried to push aside any pain. I paid attention to what was going on around me. I wanted to remember every detail.

Three days after the surgery, the wound was inspected, cleaned and exposed. Until then, it had been kept hidden under a bandage and was left undisturbed as long as no pain was felt and no discharge was observed. 'The wound looks good . . .' I was told. And then almost in disbelief I heard the words '. . . go home.' That was it?! A mere three days after having had my skull cracked open and I was allowed home.

I was surprised at first, but upon thinking about it, there was no reason why I couldn't go home. I could walk and move with almost no pain since the surgery site was on my head. I could function almost normally as long as it didn't involve aggressive movements or knocking my head, which I probably wouldn't have done even without the wound on my scalp. My husband and sons were, of course, elated at the news. Being home meant that I would be able to do my bit in packing my boys off to school the next day. After the first craniotomy, the seizures made their first appearance a few days after I was discharged and would continue daily up to the day before the second craniotomy. I will probably know soon whether the seizures will make a return.

This time, we went straight to my in-law's house before heading home. There were no whimsical stops along the way as there had been during the first surgery when I had wanted to make a pit stop for lunch first. This time, I simply wanted to be home with my family. My two boys had been with their grandparents throughout my stay in the hospital and I could not wait to be with them again. Having them visit me at the hospital was simply not the same as holding them in my arms at home. When I was there, my father-in-law asked me if he could take a look at my wound. I didn't see any reason why he shouldn't see it, so I lowered my head to bring the staples and exposed scalp into view.

The sight of it must have startled my father-in-law and he remarked in surprise, 'Oh, it's very big . . .' As before, the staples formed a C shape on top of my head from a position slightly across the centre and extending to the left. However, unlike the previous surgery, this time I did not mind others seeing it. After the aborted surgery, I had kept the scar covered even when at home. It was almost as if the scar were some taint to be ashamed of. With the second surgery, I bore that scar as a badge of honour, the physical manifestation of my will to be well again. I had also decided to be more open about my illness, my surgeries and whatever deficits, perceived or true, that came with them. I was not apologetic about it anymore. This was who I am, and it was the person that my family and I had to live with for the rest of our lives.

19

An unexpected closure

Approximately three weeks after surgery, I was back in the patient's chair. As usual, my husband was in tow. It was the second follow up—the first was about a week after the surgery and the second was about two weeks after that first appointment. The plan for that day was to discuss the results of the HPE or histopathology examination, which is doctor speak for 'let's figure out what in the world that piece of tissue we took out is'.

Whenever abnormal tissues are surgically extracted, they usually undergo microscopic analysis by pathologists. The purpose of this examination is to identify the type of tissue and then, determine whether the tissue is cancerous or merely a benign growth. If benign, then all is well and good, but if a tissue was found to be malignant or cancerous, then other steps needed to be taken.

The HPE report revealed my tumour to be a low-grade, and thus benign, type of brain tumour. In other words, it was slow growing and not cancerous. But surprise, surprise, that wasn't the end of the report. Unexpectedly, the report also mentioned the presence of another type of tissue that was rather foreign to the brain. Lodged together with the brain tumour was another piece of tissue reported as a fibroelastoma. Does that sound familiar to you? It should. The tumour that had been excised from my aortic heart valve is called a papillary fibroelastoma. Hearing that report was an epiphany for my husband and me.

I still clearly remember when my neurosurgeon tried to trace the HPE report in his clinic. Since he could not find the report among the items in my medical file, he called the pathology lab for the HPE results. I could not hear what was being said on the other end, but in the clinic, he gave us a sort of exasperated look as he replied to the person at the other end of the line, 'Yes, yes, I am a neurosurgeon and the brain is what we usually operate on.'

He gave a sort of a confused laugh and related to us that the pathologist had actually asked if he had been operating on the brain or on some other part of the body. He then explained that the pathologist had been confused because fibroelastoma tissue was not something that is supposed to be present in the brain and was thus worried that the finding had been an error. His response to the pathologist was: 'Just report it as you see it.'

When we were told that the brain tumour tissue, a type called a ganglioglioma, was found together with what appeared to be fibroelastoma tissue, it became clear what could have actually happened when I had experienced the multiple transient strokes or stroke-like episodes prior to my open-heart surgery. One probable explanation was that pieces of the papillary fibroelastoma had sheared off and had made their way via the arteries to that particular spot in the brain. It would also explain why the ultrasound images of the fibroelastoma showed that it seemed to be getting smaller and even smaller still when it was finally excised by surgery.

But if this hypothesis was true, why did it always seem to go to the same spot? The spot seen when I was diagnosed with the strokes was at approximately the same site as my tumour. During the first MRI that diagnosed the stroke, the spot had shown up as an intense glow in the imagery. A subsequent MRI then showed it to be less intense and almost disappearing into the background as expected for an infarct site after a few months. However, after almost disappearing into the background, the site took on a persistent intensity again and remained that way up to the last MRI before the brain surgery.

That was still an enigma. There were some possible explanations, but no definitive evidence to support them. As I had mentioned, the lesion site on the more recent MRIs, did not quite look like a stroke site, but my medical history indicated that I had had a previous stroke at that particular spot. Even so, the site also did not look like a typical tumour thus perhaps causing a dilemma for the surgeon as to whether he should operate on the site or not.

The HPE findings also raised a new question: did the piece of fibroelastoma get stuck because of the tumour thereby causing the strokes, or did the tumour form at the site due to the bit of fibroelastoma snagged there and irritated the surrounding brain tissue? Yes, there were these new questions. As a doctor I was curious as to what their answers may be, but what mattered the most to me was that the lesion had been removed and I had not gotten any seizures in the weeks after the surgery. The HPE results provided some closure and affirmation that I had made the right decision to proceed with all three surgeries—one open heart and two on the brain.

20

Diseases don't read textbooks

Life after the second brain surgery was blissful compared to my previous routine of daily multiple seizures. Yes, blissful, even with that huge scar on my head and even with the frequent spikes of headaches. Each day was a struggle and yet each day brought hope. The pain was still there, on some days more than others. There was no escaping it. I did undergo brain surgery after all, so yes, my head did hurt at times. However, the fact that I did not seem to be suffering from seizures anymore was perhaps more important. The sense of gloom regarding the surety of the onset of a seizure that had been shadowing my existence for the past year slowly receded as the rays of hope for the future eroded its darkness.

The number of days I was seizure free extended to become weeks. Then the weeks became months. I began to regain some sense of calmness and order in my life. Perhaps, dare I say, even a sense of normalcy. Despite this heartening progress, once you've had a seizure, you can probably never rid yourself of the foreboding sense of dread that a seizure is always a possibility. That was how badly the trauma of suffering seizures had seared into my psyche; perhaps not just for me, but also for those closest around me.

The success of the second surgery being an end to it all was what I had hoped for. Deep down, I could not shake the worry regarding the remnants of the lesion that could not be removed. Nevertheless, the fact that I was seizure free was a good thing. It also correlated the cause of the seizures to the lesion, thus meaning that my being seizure free was a sign that I could perhaps be slowly weaned off the antiepileptic drugs. It was perhaps just as well that I stopped them because I had again noticed some signs of intolerance to them.

Drug side effects are not uncommon. In fact, if one were to read the sheet of paper that accompanied the drugs, it almost seemed like every possibility under the sun was listed as a possible side effect. Some of my doctors had told me about how my case seemed particularly difficult and challenging. One factor that had caused such difficulty in treating me was my intolerance to most of the available antiepileptic medications. So, being seizure free and thus being able to taper down the drug dosage and finally stopping the antiepileptic drugs altogether was progress for not just me personally, but was probably something that my doctors considered a significant milestone for themselves as well.

The complexity of my case had been compounded by symptoms or presentations that kept evolving, sometimes almost on a daily basis. It had come to a point when one day, I related some new set of symptoms during a clinic follow up and was taken aback by the lack of interest evinced by the medical officer. My first thought was that the symptoms I was reporting were probably rather common, so it was not something that the doctor had not heard before. Then, the doctor simply said that I was not supposed to be having those symptoms.

That struck me as odd. Did the doctor think I was lying or making things up? Then it occurred to me what might have been happening. I don't think the doctor thought I was lying, but what I was relating somehow did not tally with what is available in some medical textbook, therefore what I was reporting was not what I should have been reporting. It seemed strange at first to have been dismissed in such a way. But I would later find out from my interactions with others that it was not really an uncommon experience. Others had also been told that the symptoms they were reporting were wrong or did not tally with their diagnosis. It seemed a strange response after going through the trouble of asking the patient to relate their medical history and report symptoms only to tell the patient that it did not fit the textbook for the patient's diagnosis and therefore the patient was probably wrong.

Most of this over-dependence on correlating symptoms to what is inscribed in a medical textbook seemed to occur with the more junior doctors, perhaps stemming from a lack of experience. There was even one point, when I was having a seizure and which my husband recognized as one and called in a medical officer, who dismissed it as 'not a seizure' because it did not fit into what he understood to be a generalized seizure. It was very disturbing for me to be told that whatever I was reporting did not fit my diagnosis and therefore probably wrong.

On one such frustrating occasion, I related it to my friend, who had also suffered a sudden serious illness and complications from that illness. She herself was a doctor, more senior than I was and had been similarly dismissed once; even laughed at and told that whatever she was saying couldn't have possibly happened despite her having evidence of the fact. She consoled me by saying something simple yet insightful and deep: 'Diseases don't read textbooks.' How right she was. This is perhaps an important aspect of the practice of medicine that needs to be addressed.

It is not my intention to scare patients into thinking that they will be mismanaged. What I want to point out is that the over reliance on a reference for what constitutes as normal and what should be considered abnormal, is perhaps not the best way to practise medical decision-making in the current day and age. I agree that reference points are necessary; but the doctor also has the reference point of the patient in person, or a trusted caregiver.

I remember a remark that my neurosurgeon made to a group of medical students present during a clinic follow up, 'In medicine, communication is most important.' I remember that I couldn't help myself from nodding in agreement when he said it. The human species consists of billions of individuals, no two alike, not even in the case of identical twins. It seems quite a folly to think that afflictions affecting them could be rigidly categorized as if the human race had one representative individual for whom the physiology could be referenced as normal. It is also quite absurd to assume that a disease would have read a medical textbook and would therefore merely confine its behaviour and symptoms to what was expected of it as had been written in the texts.

So, am I saying that doctors shouldn't use textbooks or reference materials? No, definitely not. This is where communication becomes an indispensable component of practising medicine. Obviously, textbooks and references are a necessity for disseminating knowledge—I am not trying to dispute that. However, when a doctor interacts with a patient, there are additional sources of information in the form of what the patients and their caregivers are able to convey—this is an invaluable resource that provides the doctor with objectivity regarding a particular case.

Other than the actual clinical work such as diagnosis and treatment either by drugs or surgery, communication is probably the next most important aspect of practising medicine. Unfortunately, a medical practitioner's ability to communicate with patients is perhaps almost never properly assessed throughout a doctor's training from medical school onwards. It doesn't matter whether the patient is a doctor or not, what you want is a doctor who can communicate well with all patients from all backgrounds.

Unfortunately, there are still some doctors who are rather lacking in the communication skills department. My interactions with these doctors caused me a rather great amount of stress. As I had mentioned, my symptoms and list of complaints kept on changing. When I had to see other doctors, who were not primarily treating me, among the responses that I received were:

'Well, you've just had surgery, of course you should have pain in *so and so* place . . .'

And it would end there without any further examination or investigation since the assumption had already taken root.

'Are you under any stress? Is there anything new that is stressing you?' This usually happened when the doctor had read the part in the case notes that mention my non-epileptic seizures; in this case, the assumption was probably that my pain or seizures were psychologically caused by stress and it would also end there without any further examination or investigation.

'No other patient has complained of that before.' This type of response would usually stop me in my tracks. If I was still talking about any particular symptoms, I would simply say okay and silently wish for the session to end as quickly as possible. With this sort of response, I get the feeling that either the doctor is of the opinion that I am just being difficult and complaining about every little discomfort, or that I was exaggerating which explained why no one has had a similar complaint previously.

This was the situation that I had found myself in. I had reached a point where at times I wondered whether I should even bother to go to any of the clinic follow ups. I would argue with my husband that there was no point since it was just a matter of my being brushed off or told to continue as previously, with the implied message that I am complaining too much and should perhaps be more grateful for my current state of health since there were many others so much worse off than I was.

Perhaps I have a low pain threshold and am a rather difficult patient who complains a lot. Or maybe even my expectations of recovery are too high that I keep thinking I should have no deficits or lingering pain at all. I do admit to all this and do not squarely put the blame on the way some of these doctors had responded. I just wished that their message could have been communicated in a gentler way that took into consideration the sensitivities of the patient, me. I must also admit, although I do not recall any specific case, perhaps I too had been guilty of treating my patients in such a brusque way. So, being a patient was definitely a wake-up call that I hope has in turn made me a better doctor.

For me, writing was a form of therapy. When I was no longer involved in any clinical work, writing also became a means of practising medicine. Through my writing, I could reach out and educate about illnesses and practices. I needed the credentials of being a medical doctor and the experience of practising medicine so that I could help many others in ways that I could not by merely practising out of a clinic.

As much as I loved practising clinical medicine, writing was perhaps my calling and all the various detours the journey of my life had taken thus far converged to this point. My experience has given me insights into how medicine being practised is very specialized, focused on the deep minutiae, but at times lacking the big picture and how, despite the billions of humans, we use a somewhat rigid reference of what is considered normal.

Diseases are complex and tend to affect multiple systems. For example, a disease like diabetes is an endocrine (hormone) system problem, but it can also affect the eyes, the kidneys, can cause long chronic infections that can lead to tissue death that may in turn require surgical intervention such as amputations of the affected regions. The disease can also affect cardiovascular health. Imagine how many specialist doctors a long-term diabetic patient may end up needing to see.

Having all the experts in very particular specializations or sub-specializations is a good thing—don't get me wrong. But it can be very daunting for a patient to navigate the complexities of the healthcare infrastructure. Even the medical terminology can be confusing and intimidating to many. For example, there are ophthalmologists, optometrists and opticians—are they the same or different? Who should the patients see and what do they say to each different one? How can patients communicate more effectively with the doctors and vice versa, how can the doctors communicate more effectively with their patients?

These are the issues that I wanted to take up and address. I realized how important it is to treat the patients as individuals. Doctors, including myself, are perhaps rather too dependent on medical texts and references and sometimes fail to use our own judgement and logic to assess a particular situation on its own without trying to fit it into an expected mould.

21

A consequence of sequence

After graduation from medical school, I began my career as a house officer or houseman, the required step before being able to obtain a full license to practise medicine. This stage is equivalent to that of a medical intern in systems like the ones in the United States. House officers are required to do several postings in various departments as part of the post-medical-school, clinical training.

I am not really sure if I had ever envisioned myself as a medical doctor when I was in school. As a result of my interest in art and drawing, I had thought of taking up architecture as a profession. But somehow, the influence of others around me, and the fact that I found myself in a matriculation system that provided no access to an architecture degree programme, led me to medical school. My early days in medical school were difficult, exciting, confusing and exhausting all rolled into one. There was so much to read and do and there did not seem to be much time for anything else.

Upon graduation, I was still very much unsure of what specialty I wanted to pursue and whether I even wanted to take up a specialty. My housemanship included postings in the orthopaedics department as well as the obstetrics and gynaecology department. These postings were a revelation in the sense that it became clear to me I did not want to take up those specialties. Again, circumstances sort of made the decision for me.

After my housemanship, I was allowed to continue as a medical officer (MO) in the same hospital as per my request. I had been informed that I was to report as an MO with the Otorhinolaryngology Department otherwise known as the ENT department (for ear, nose, throat). Otorhinolaryngology was not one of the postings that house officers were required to undergo, so I had no prior hands-on clinical experience with that sort of work. As it turned out, ENT work was something that I found compatible with me.

When I had had enough service experience and was eligible for postgraduate medical school, it was an obvious choice that I applied to further my training to become an ENT surgeon by registering to do my Master's in Surgery (Otorhinolaryngology and Head and Neck Surgery). It was also during my stint in the ENT department that I got married and my eldest son was born. About halfway through my ENT postgraduate training, my husband had to leave and work in Sheffield, England. I was not able to immediately accompany him due to work commitments and was only able to join him about eighteen months later.

Prior to leaving for Sheffield, an accident befell my elder son. The accident left me so traumatized that I decided to not continue with my ENT training in order to spend time with him and care for him better. Although I had enjoyed the work in otorhinolaryngology, especially doing the fine surgeries in the head and neck area, I decided that, with my husband being away, our son's wellbeing was more important than my potential career as a surgeon. I made the decision to leave my postgraduate training. A few months later, I was able to join my husband in the United Kingdom.

At first, I was uncertain about how I would be able to cope with spending all day at home. As it turned out, I found the whole experience very rewarding. I was at home with my two boys on a full-time basis. They were too young for school at the time. Except for naps and the times that they were amusing themselves with various toys or books (this was before the days of smartphones and tablets), they would spend the whole working day interacting with me.

After returning to Malaysia, I resumed practising medicine. Less than a month after returning to work, my younger son fell ill. I made the decision to resign from my permanent hospital position. Official documents pertaining to my employment were signed and that was it—I was a doctor without any means of practising medicine. But I had other things to worry about.

As my younger son's health improved over the period of a year, I accepted *locum* jobs—standing in for the regular doctors at a general practice clinic in my neighbourhood and at a friend's practice once a week. This was my first real taste of general practice. I felt that being the neighbourhood doctor suited me. Despite being very much an introverted person, talking to patients and educating them about their health was something I enjoyed. When the opportunity to start my own general practice presented itself, I jumped in without hesitation.

All these decisions led me to that fateful day in my clinic. I was running a high fever that was diagnosed to be a stroke caused by a heart tumour. This led to the open-heart surgery to remove the tumour.

Although I was a patient throughout the strokes and heart surgery, the doctor in me felt that I had to keep notes. If it was fated that I would succumb to my illness, I wanted my sons to know what had happened to me. I also saw it as an opportunity to reach out and educate others about heart surgery, a procedure that we are seeing a rise of globally. Despite being a medical doctor, I was filled with apprehension and dread regarding the surgery. I struggled with the post-op recovery. I wanted others to know that it was in a way a normal part of the whole process. It was okay to have those struggles. The important thing was to grow from it.

Those notes had led to my first book being published. But, as you now know, my story did not end there although I so very much wished to not have written this second book. Soon after the book *The Doctor is Sick* was published. I was scheduled for a second brain surgery; the first brain surgery had taken place just before the manuscript had been accepted for publication. As a result, the book did not have any launch event. Instead, the book quietly took its place among the other books on the store shelves.

I did have my own little personal ritual though. Well, it is my first book after all. I couldn't exactly let it go out into the world just like that without doing anything. The thrill and excitement of seeing your book on the shelves for the first time is something that probably every author will go through. So, I went with my family and we took pictures with the book whichever store shelves we could find it on. And that was our little family ritual.

The elation of seeing one's writing evolve from assorted compiled nonsensical scribbles to a bound tome on the shelves in bookstores is rather hard to describe. It is only an experience that someone who has published can relate to. There is a fulfilling sense of accomplishment. Yes, it is possible that the book might just sell four copies ever. But that does not matter to you when you see them sitting on the shelf in the store.

There is also a sense of gratitude that comes with publishing what you hope will be a good book for the readers. The finished product on display had been proofread numerous times, edited, commented on and refined by the editors. Then there were the many nameless individuals who were just as crucial, the graphics team and other jobs I may have never even heard of, each of them a critical component in the conveyor belt from my writing to the store shelves.

For me, publishing a book was a childhood dream come true. As a child growing up, I was not well to do. Having said that, although life was hard, I had never really felt underprivileged. To think so would demean the efforts of my late father in providing and caring for my siblings and me. We did not have much in the way of material wealth, but I cannot say that we were unhappy. When it came to books, we simply could not afford to buy any.

Growing up in an agrarian community in Malaysia in the late 1970s and the 1980s, my only contact with books were the school textbooks, and those that were publicly available in the little mobile community library—a caravan that functioned as an extension of the public library for rural communities. It only became natural that I saw books as a source of knowledge and wonder and thus dreamed of the day that perhaps I too would proudly look upon a cover with my name on it.

Now, the book was no longer just an assortment of notes on scrap paper and in various notebooks anymore. It was an actual bound book with an ISBN number and all. But there was also a certain melancholy associated with the realization that my book was actually published. Was that my mark on the world? Was that the only mark that people would remember me by? Was that my first and last book? Perhaps one does tend to get a bit morbid and think about these things when facing a major operation like brain surgery.

But the story about the first book did not simply end with it getting on the book store shelves. It went on to win an *Anugerah Buku Negara* 2017 (The National Book Award) category. Surprised. Thankful. Those are just two of the words that describe how I felt when I saw the notification email. So why was I surprised at winning the award? Well, if the answer was not obvious enough, it is mainly the fact that it was my first book. I had not done anything like that before.

Sure, I had written some public education articles for health magazines, but that was a very different process. I went through the whole book-publishing process in an almost trancelike manner. I don't think I had any real idea of what I was doing when I had sent the manuscript to the publisher. Despite that, I think I was quite driven into writing and eventually into getting the book on to the store shelves and into the hands of readers. In a way, I partly considered the effort as part of my legacy.

I was also surprised to know about winning the award simply because I had expected other more worthy and talented writers to win it. My surprise did not come from total ignorance. I was actually aware that the book had been nominated for the award. But at that time, I was still very much in spread-the-word mode. I guess I still am and I hope to always be. I want as many people as possible to read the book. Giving out ten copies of the book for the review process when nominated simply meant that ten more people read the book. Ten more people who might benefit from my experience and pass on what they had read to their friends and family—a multiplier effect of sorts. It even came to a point where I even gave copies away whenever I could afford it to those who I felt might benefit from reading it.

Writing the book to tell my story was not about taking advantage of my misfortune to gain sympathy. I felt that it was a story I needed to tell and to educate others in my own way. There are many other books out there about struggles with various illnesses, even those written by other doctors. However, many of these books were about cancer and some were written by terminal patients.

I wanted to write about a journey of self-discovery and personal struggle that I felt could be similar to the experiences of many other individuals out there who thought they were suffering alone and in silence. The illness was a mere trigger to set me off on my journey. I did not want anyone to feel sorry for me. I remember some of the feedback I had gotten from readers of *The Doctor is Sick* who personally knew me—they related to me how they had teared up even on the first few pages of the book. That rather caught me by surprise. I had no intention for the book to be a tear-jerker. I wanted the book to pass on many messages, but to solicit sympathy for me was definitely never an objective.

It was supposed to be a book celebrating the knowledge and technological prowess of the human species—the advanced medical imaging capability combined with surgical intervention and drugs that extended my time on this Earth. It was a book about hope—despite my despair about the illness. I had struggled and hopefully triumphed to carry on with life and it was proof that the light is there at the end of the tunnel, if only we could patiently bear with it and push through the darkness. It was a book celebrating life and how precious and transient our existence in this world is. It was a book about the compassion of the many kind-hearted souls who had touched my life and made it better—my family, friends, doctors, caregivers and anyone who simply wished me well.

No, I am not naive or super-idealistic (at least I hope not). If the book sold well and made some money—that was nice, great even. I definitely did not have the funds, time or resources to publish a book and distribute it. So, yes, the book needed to be sold so that some money could be made, as at least some form of return for the publishers who had taken a chance on an unknown author with no publishing experience like me. Well, while we're on the subject, let me sincerely thank you for buying this book!

There are many out there who have had their well-planned routes in life disrupted by diseases or other changes and personal tragedies. Many others, like me, had a less well-planned route, but nevertheless a general direction in mind.

We adapted to the changes and bends in the road. Even so, the impact of such disruptions is not necessarily diminished by any degree. The journey of life is full of unexpected twists, forks and obstructions—one does not have to be a great philosopher to arrive at that conclusion. But what do we make of these disruptions and how do we adapt to them?

I believe that life abounds with opportunities. Yes, we can make plans, but those plans can come to nought at the most unexpected of times. I believe that at every point of disruption, there is an opportunity to move forward. These disruptions have been ordained by fate. But the choices that we make in choosing an opportunity for growth and progress, as opposed to falling into despair and inertia, will be what define the rest of our lives. Looking back on my own journey thus far, I can put it all into context.

I was not meant to be an architect. I was meant to go to medical school and become a doctor. But I was not meant to be a surgeon. Had I taken that route, I might have despaired later when my medical problems would force me to abandon the practice of surgery. I had aspired to be an author, but never would I have envisioned that being a doctor who was suddenly taken ill would have been the route to publish my first book.

I had suffered strokes, had surgery for a heart tumour and then discovered that the site of the stroke also had a brain tumour. I shudder to think of the outcomes if I had been diagnosed with a brain tumour and had undergone the brain surgery first. It simply meant that I would then still have had the possibility of suffering strokes because the heart tumour had gone undetected.

That in turn meant I might still have had to undergo heart surgery and possibly even another brain surgery. Or it was also quite possible that the strokes could have been more damaging. Perhaps worse than that was if the heart tumour had been left undetected because the problem was believed to have been resolved. The strokes caused by it could have simply been attributed to complications or long-term damage associated with the brain surgery and not investigated further. At times, the twists and turns of fate have an order to them that is far beyond the comprehension of mere mortals.

I am under no illusions that I will live to a ripe old age, although I just might, such is the nature of fate. I hope that I am able to appreciate whatever moments I have left knowing fully well that the countdown had started. We often forget that the countdown to our demise begins at the moment that we breathe our first as we exit the womb into this world. Unfortunately, worldly pleasures and pursuits serve as distractions that silence the ticking of the seconds as they pass by.

What differentiates bad decisions from what is fated? There are those who believe that the direction our lives take is fully in our hands and determined by the decisions we make. For me, the dawn of each new day, is a reminder that my extended time in this transient existence that we call life has been the consequence of a sequence of events and decisions. Our life may be but an insignificant speck in time, but we can decide to make that speck as significant as possible. For a period, I had a life that was a process of not dying. Now, I will live each day like my last—a life of love, faith and personal triumphs.